THE ROYAL TIGER OF BENGAL

"I shot the brute in 1861, when encamped at the village of Mutteeara. A cow had been killed across the river, and I took my elephants over at once and found him very soon, disabling him with one shot. There was nothing interesting about his death, except his enormous size. He was over 12 feet as he lay, and his skin thrown loosely over two charpoys, placed *lengthways*, covered both completely! It measured 13 ft. 5 in. or 6 in. pegged out. He was incomparably the largest tiger I have ever seen."

LIEUT.-COL. BOILEAU.

THE ROYAL TIGER OF BENGAL

HIS LIFE AND DEATH

J. FAYRER

ISBN : 978-93-5324-557-3 (HB)

First Published, London, 1875

Published, 2020

Published by

Facsimile Publisher
12 Pragati Market
Ashok Vihar, Ph-2
Delhi-110052
E-mail: books@facsimilepublisher.com

Printed at: G. Print Process, Delhi.

The Royal tiger of Bengal

Author: J. Fayrer

THE

ROYAL TIGER OF BENGAL

HIS LIFE AND DEATH

BY

J. FAYRER, M.D. F.Z.S.

BENGAL MEDICAL SERVICE

LONDON

J. & A. CHURCHILL, NEW BURLINGTON STREET

—

1875

TO

LIEUT.-COL. G. W. BOILEAU, BENGAL ARMY

In reminiscence of a Tiger-shooting Party

In the Oude Terai

ERRATA.

Page 2, place "Tribe Digitigrada," *below* "Order Carnivora."

Page 2, line 4, "Placentaria," *should be* "Placentalia."

Page 25, line 11, "Cervus muntjac," *should be* "Cervulus vaginalis." "Rusa aristotelii," line 12, *should be* "Cervus aristotelis." "Rucervus duvaucelii," *should be* "Cervus duvaucelli." "Portax picta," line 13, *should be* "Boselaphus pictus."

Page 32, line 3, "(P. mollurus)," *should be* "(P. molurus)."

Page 50, last line, "Seesoo," *should be* "Sissoo."

Page 75, last line but one, "Dalbergia sisoo," *should be* "Dalbergia sissoo."

Page 84, last line but two, "(entellus)," *should be* "(semnopithecus entellus)."

Page 93, line 24, "putiah," *should be* "putial."

SEE PAGE 3.

There is one animal very nearly allied to the cats, named Cryptoprocta Ferox, found in Madagascar. It is described in "Recherches sur la faune de Madagascar," by Pollen and Schlegei, also by A. Milne Edwardes.

THE ROYAL TIGER OF BENGAL.

IN the following pages it is proposed to give a sketch of the natural history and habits of the largest and most powerful of the cat tribe, which from its size, strength, ferocity, and beauty, claims supremacy over all congeners, not excepting even the lion, and is, therefore, well entitled to the epithet "Royal," bestowed by naturalists.

Having seen something of the tiger in his home, and not unfrequently encountered him in his native swamps and jungle, the description will involve not merely a zoological definition, but also an account of his habits and mode of life, as well as of his death.

The purpose is, in short, to consider him from a field naturalist's point of view.

It may be well to begin by stating the tiger's position in the scale of animal life.

It is of the—

SUB-KINGDOM . . .	*Vertebrata.*
CLASS	*Mammalia.*
SUB-CLASS	*Placentaria.*
TRIBE	*Digitigrada.*
ORDER	*Carnivora.*
FAMILY	*Felidæ.*
GENUS	*Felis.*
SPECIES	*Felis Tigris Linn., or T. Regalis of Gray.*

A few words in explanation of this formula may not be out of place.

The tiger is a vertebrate animal, whose embryonic development is allantoid and placental; a warm-blooded, air-breathing creature that suckles its young until they are old enough to follow their carnivorous instincts and eat flesh; having all the ordinary characters of other mammals with certain modifications, which adapt it to its predatory and carnivorous life, and place it in the feline family of which it is a typical exemplar. It is unnecessary to enter into details of the characteristics of the sub-kingdom, class, and order to which this family belongs; but it may be well to state briefly those of the family itself.

The felidæ are the typical carnivores; they are distinguished by a rounded head, short but powerful jaws, armed with formidable fangs and cutting teeth. They have vigorous limbs, digitigrade feet armed with sharp retractile claws, and cushioned with soft pads on the under surface, which aid in giving the noiseless, stealthy tread and vigorous spring. Active by night and day, vision is adapted for either, the pupil dilates widely in a feeble, while it contracts to a vertical slit, or minute point, in a bright light. Hearing is acute; speed, strength, and agility remarkable. The tongue covered with sharp recurved firm, long papillæ, which give it a rasp-like appearance, and by which the remaining flesh, that has escaped the teeth, is licked from the bones of its prey. The clavicles, or collar-bones, are very small and rudimentary, lying imbedded in the well-developed muscles near the shoulder.

The felidæ are distributed generally over the globe, except in Australia and Madagascar; but the species with which we are concerned is limited entirely to Asia. The Asiatic cats or felidæ were divided by Blyth into three groups,—the pardine, the lynxine and the cheetah (F. jubata). A popular subdivision is into lions, tigers, leopards, cats, and lynxes. The cheetah (F. jubata), or hunting leopard, though associated in this arrangement with the Felis pardus, or leopard, differs considerably from that animal. The general appearance of the tiger is so familiar that it seems almost superfluous to describe it. Its figure denotes a combination of great strength, suppleness, and agility,—the elongated, lithe, at the same time deep and compressed body; the comparatively short but vigorous limbs, with their elastic cushioned digitigrade feet, sharp retractile claws, and powerful muscles which attain their greatest development in the region of the jaw, neck, shoulder and forearm, and the formidable fangs, all proclaim a predatory blood-thirsty creature, armed and fitted to wage war against and maintain supremacy over other animals.

Before proceeding further with that which concerns the natural history, it may be well to give a short description of the modifications of the mammalian structure, which peculiarly characterize the tiger and fit him for his predatory life. These are certain points in connection with the structure of the head, jaws and teeth—the muscular, osseous, and digestive systems.

The skull of the tiger is adapted for the insertion and action of powerful muscles and teeth. The tentorium or septum that separates the cerebrum from the cerebellum, and which in man and many other creatures is membranous, is bony in the felidæ, probably for the purpose of increasing the strength of the skull, and not, as has been suggested, for the purpose of diminishing the shock of cerebrum against cerebellum in the feline leaps and bounds; for which purpose, indeed, the elastic membranous tentorium would answer better. The lower jaw is short and strong, and is articulated to the skull by a hinge-like joint, which restricts its movements nearly in a vertical plane—that of opening and closing the mouth. The coronoid process, which gives insertion to the temporal muscles, is proportionately large. The muscles are all very powerful, and arise from large and deep fossæ, which have well-marked ridges of bone. The zygomas form expanded arches, under which the temporal muscles pass, and they give attachment to certain bundles of muscular fibres. The masseter muscles, which aid the temporals in the

Fig. 1.

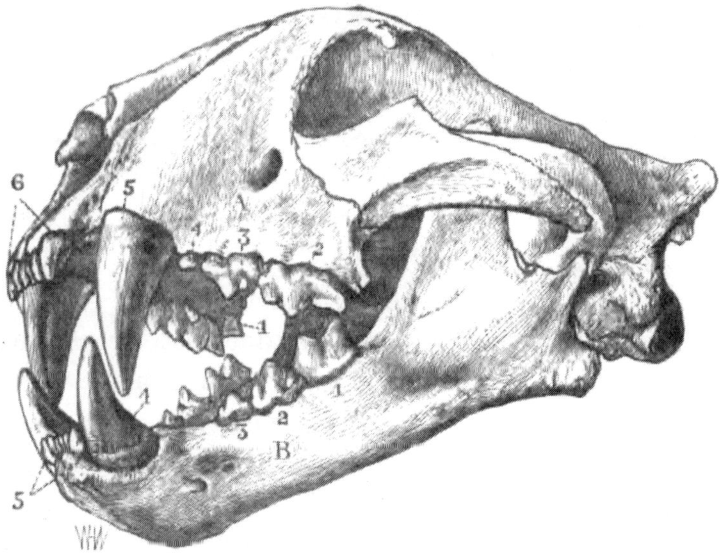

DENTITION OF TIGER.

A, Upper Jaw:—1, Molar; 2, Premolar, sectorial; 3, Premolar; 4, Premolar; 5, Canine or Laniary; 6, Incisors.

B, Lower Jaw:—1, Molar, sectorial; 2, Premolar; 3, Premolar; 4, Canine or Laniary; 5, Incisors.

movements of the lower jaw, are also large, whilst the pterygoids are relatively small. The teeth are of the diphyodont type; that is, they are first deciduous and then permanent. They are firmly implanted in deep sockets in the jaws, and consist of dentine, enamel, and crusta petrosa. They have special forms, entirely adapted for flesh-eating. In each jaw there are six incisors, the outermost resembling a small canine tooth, and two long and powerful canine or holding teeth or laniaries; these, which are enormously developed, are the formidable fangs, and are pointed, recurved, convex, and grooved in front, and sharp-edged behind. The lower canines are rather smaller than, and pass in front of, the upper when the mouth is closed. The molars, or cheek teeth, are eight in number in the upper jaw, the first being only rudimentary, and has no corresponding tooth in the lower jaw. There are six in the lower jaw. The second tooth in both upper and lower jaw has a conical crown and two roots. The third upper tooth has a cutting crown with three pointed lobes and a flat inner side, against which the cutting teeth in the lower jaw works obliquely. There is a small tubercular tooth behind and on the inner side of the upper tooth. These tuberculated cutting teeth are called sectorial, "dents carnassières" of Cuvier. They are seen in their most characteristic form in the tiger.

The formula is—

$$\text{Incisors } \frac{3\cdot3}{3\cdot3}; \text{ Canines } \frac{1\cdot1}{1\cdot1}; \text{ Premolars } \frac{3\cdot3}{2\cdot2}; \text{ Molars } \frac{1\cdot1}{1\cdot1} \text{ 30.}$$

The purpose of these teeth is obvious. The small incisors are used to gnaw the soft ends of bones, and to scrape off fibrous and tendinous structures. The long fang-like canines seize, pierce, and hold the prey. The sectorial, or scissor-like teeth, working vertically against each other, serve to cut and divide the flesh or to crush the bones. These movements being effected by powerful muscles, which pass under the zygomatic arches from high crests of bone on the boldly-sculptured skull, and give the peculiar aspect so characteristic of the carnivora. The tiger has a moderately well-developed brain of the gyrencephalic type; that is to say, the cerebral lobes are convoluted, and extend somewhat over the cerebellum, from which they are separated by the bony tentorium, and are united transversely by a corpus callosum. The special senses of hearing and vision are acute, whilst smell seems to be comparatively defective. The pupils are round, in which respect they differ from some other cats, which have vertical pupils; the tapetum lucidum is of a greenish hue, which gives the eye a peculiar and characteristic glare when the pupil is dilated, and is often well seen in the wounded tiger when crouching preparatory to a charge. The tactile sensibility is acute, and is especially marked in the so-called whiskers upon the chin, lips, cheeks, and eyebrows. Each hair has extreme sensibility at its root, and is moveable by muscular fibres which form a portion of the platysma myoïdes, and surround the hair bulb, which is connected with a bed of glands and with the nerves of the lip. They are, no doubt, of use as feelers in their stealthy movements by night and day. It is not only in the jaws that the muscular development is so remarkable, but also in the neck, shoulder, and forearm. The whole muscular system is, indeed, highly developed, but it is especially so in the above-mentioned sites as contrasted with that of the hinder extremities. The tiger can not only strike down a cow or even a buffalo with his forearm and paw, and hold it with the long fangs which his powerful jaws enable him to imbed in the flesh of his struggling victim, but can also raise it from the ground through the action of the powerful muscles of the neck, which take their origin from the vertebral spines, and can either carry or drag it off to his lair, where he devours it at leisure.

Those who have seen the tiger when stripped of his skin, can hardly fail to have been struck with the grotesque resemblance to a gigantic human form which is presented by his sinewy and muscular frame as the arms are stretched out on either side. The vast shoulder, arm, forearm, wrist, and hand have a wonderfully anthropoid appearance.

It is sufficient to say that these muscles are modifications of those in the human or other mammalian limbs, and that they attain the excessive development in obedience to the necessities of the creature's existence.

The distal phalanges and their claws are remarkable, and may be briefly mentioned. There are five in each fore, and four in each hind foot. The mechanism by which they are made retractile is interesting. The claw and the phalanx into which it is fitted are kept in the retracted position by an elastic ligament, which connects the two phalanges.

FIG. 2.

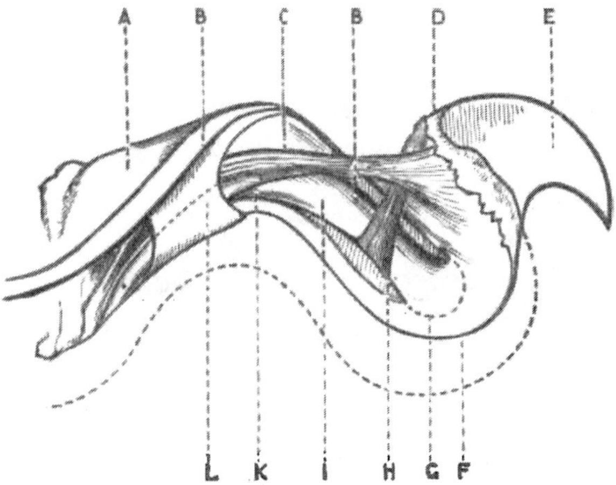

FELINE CLAW OF FORE FOOT PARTLY EXTENDED.

A, Proximal phalanx. B B, Extensor-tendon, helps to exsert and steadies the claw. C, Lateral ligament. D, Fold of claw sheath. E, The claw. F, Distal phalanx. G, Flexor perforans. H, Elastic ligament. I, Second phalanx. K, Flexor perforatus. L, Annular ligament.

It is unsheathed by the action of a flexor muscle (flexor profundus), which opposes the action of the ligament, and can be exerted at will. The claw phalanx when retracted by the ligament is drawn to the outer or ulnar side of the second phalanx, not *on* to it, the joint that connects them being so formed as to admit of this oblique action. By this arrangement the claws during ordinary progression are withdrawn, and kept out of the way, and are consequently not liable to wear or be blunted by contact with the ground. When the tiger wishes he can, by an exertion of the flexor profundus, exsert the claws and use them as formidable weapons. Owen ("Comp. Anat. and Physiol.," p. 69, 70, vol. iii.), says, "The toes of the hind foot are retracted in a different direction, viz., directly upon, not by the sides of the second phalanges, and the elastic ligaments are differently disposed."

This, if it be the case in the lion and tiger and larger felidæ, is not so in ocelots and other small cats, in which the arrangement is very like that of the fore foot. It may be that, as climbers, they require

FIG. 3.

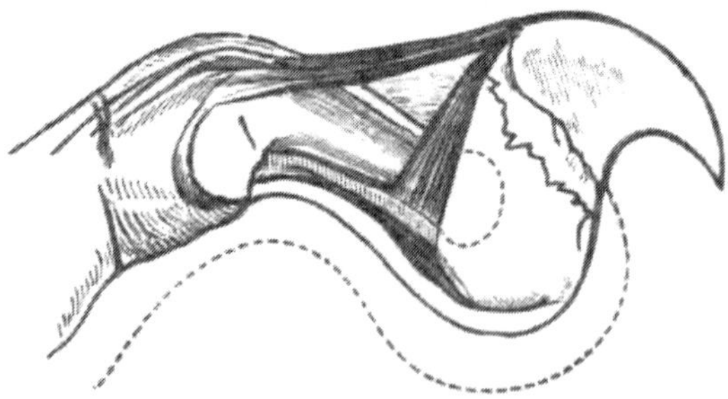

CLAW OF HIND FOOT.

as great strength and retractility in the hind as in the fore claws.

The skeleton of the tiger is remarkable for the perfection of its mechanism. The bones are compact, dense, and strong. The trunk is comparatively slender, the simple digestive apparatus of the carnivora requiring little space. Lightness and gracefulness of the body, with great agility and speed, are thus secured, being needed in the extensive leaps that the tiger, though in a less degree than the other felidæ, is wont to make.

The stomach and alimentary tract correspond to the teeth. Digestion of the warm flesh, sometimes hardly dead before being swallowed, is very easy. The stomach is simple, and the intestine short, the colon and cæcum being remarkably so, and in this respect very different to those of herbivorous animals. This allows of a small abdominal cavity, and consequent lightness of the body.

The clavicles are rudimentary, and lie imbedded in the muscles of the anterior part of the shoulder. They are frequently lost in dissecting the animal, unless looked for carefully. They are regarded as charms and amulets by the natives in India.

From this slight sketch of the anatomy, we will pass on to study the tiger from other points of view.

Contrary to custom, I propose to give him precedence of the lion. He is generally described as inferior, though nearly equal, to the so-called king of beasts; but in size, strength, activity, and beauty he really surpasses him, and, therefore, though he may neither be so courageous nor so dignified, he is entitled to the first place—at all events, in India—

for there he is in his home, whilst the lion, comparatively rare and confined to certain limited portions of India, such as Guzerat, Gwalior, and a few other localities, is, as it were, the outlying and degenerate representative of a branch of a fauna that attains its highest development in Africa; withal, the largest tiger exceeds the largest lion in size as much as in strength and activity. The lion is indebted, to a certain extent, to his noble head and mane for the dignity of his appearance, and for an apparent exaggeration of his real size. The absence of this ornament in the tiger makes him contrast in this respect unfavourably, but a comparison of the largest specimens of each, despoiled of their skins, would decide the question in favour of the tiger. I have measured them as they lay dead on the spot where they had fallen, more than ten feet from the nose to the end of the tail, and there is little doubt that they exceed even this length; now, as no lion has ever attained such a size, the question must be decided in favour of the tiger, so far as size and strength are concerned. In ferocity he cannot be exceeded; whether the evidences of a more noble and generous nature sometimes ascribed to the lion are really genuine, may be doubted. If true, may they not be the result of a more apathetic and less energetically savage nature, which, in this respect, makes the lion appear a more amiable savage than the tiger.

There is only one species of tiger, though there

are several varieties in colour and even shape; some are longer and lighter, often shorter, proportionately higher, and have both limbs and body of more bulky development than others. The colour of a full grown tiger in good health is exceedingly beautiful. The ground is of a rufous, or tawny yellow, shaded into white on the ventral surface. This is varied with vertical black stripes, or elongated ovals and brindlings. On the face and posterior surface of the ears the white markings are peculiarly well defined, and present an appearance as remarkable as beautiful. The depth of shade of the ground colour, and the intensity of the black markings vary, according to the age and condition of the animal. In old tigers the ground becomes more tawny, of a lighter shade, and the black markings better defined. The young are more dusky in the ground colouring than the middle-aged or old tigers.

The depth of colour is also affected by locality and climate; those found in forests are often of a deeper shade than tigers found in more open localities. It is said that in more northern latitudes they are of a lighter colour, almost white. The circular white patches on the back of the ears, and the white and black about the face are very conspicuous in the tiger rushing through the grass or jungle, when disturbed. Brilliant as is the general colour, it is remarkable how well it harmonizes with the grass or bush, among which he prowls, and for which indeed, until his charge and the short deep growls or barkings which accompany it, reveal his presence, he may be mistaken. The tigress differs from the tiger; the head, as well as the whole body, is smaller and narrower. The neck is lighter, and is devoid of any crest, which though very much smaller than the voluminous mane of the lion, undoubtedly exists in large and old males. The tigress is lither, more active, and when accompanied by her offspring far more savage and blood-thirsty than the male; she will then attack, even when unprovoked, and in defence of her young, of which she is proverbially fond, is as courageous as she is vicious. Most of the accidents that have befallen sportsmen and others who have encountered these animals have been due to tigresses. I have seen a tigress, accompanied by her young, charge, unprovoked, a line of elephants, and inflict severe injuries before she was despatched. The only well-authenticated case in which a sportsman was taken out of a howdah was one in which a tigress, in one bound, reached the sportsman, her hind feet resting on the elephant's head—the fore feet on the rail of the howdah. The occupant, who had mortally wounded her as she sprang, was seized, and, after a short struggle, dragged or thrown to the ground. The tigress then received another bullet, and died where she fell; the sportsman, severely wounded, was carried into camp, and slowly recovered from the injuries, which were severe. This occurred to the well-known Colonel

H——, and the scene of the adventure was in the Oude Terai, where it was witnessed by one of the party, from whom I received the description. I have seen a tigress, unaccompanied by her young, deeply lacerate the heads of two and the hind quarters of a third elephant, severely injuring a mahout by tearing his leg with one of the fore paws, in the space of a few minutes, before she was placed *hors-de-combat*. This exciting incident took place in Purneah, in Bengal, and the scene of it was a large tract of long fine grass, in which she could not be seen until she charged and seized the elephants. In this case the cubs were probably not far distant.

As a general rule, the first instinct of the hunted tiger is to escape his pursuers, and as he is very wary, much skill and management are needed to prevent him from doing so. He will creep stealthily out of the corner of the cover, and slip away unseen, if not watched, at the different outlets or nákas. The only chance of securing is to wound him; he will then, generally, turn and fight, charge repeatedly at the nearest object, until he is disabled, and incapable of fighting any longer.

The tiger has synonyms, according to his habitat. In Bengal and some other parts of India he is known as Bagh; the Tigress Baghni—sometimes Sela-Bagh, or Go-Bagh. In the North by the Persian name Shér—female, Shérni;—according to Jerdon, in Bundelkund and Central India, Nahar.—

By the Southals and Hill people about Bhaugulpore, Tút;—by some, Pulung;—in Goruckpore he is known as Nungya-char. In the Tamul and Telogoo tongues he is Pali-Reddapúli;—in Malabar, Parampúli;—by the Canarese, Huli. In Thibet, he is Tágh; in the Lepcha country, Sahtong;—in Bhotanese he is Túkt; in Burmese, Kya; in Chinese, Lau-chu, or Lau-hu. The common name for tiger in Bengal, Oude, and the North-west is Bagh, or Shér. The lion being known as Bubher Shér, or Untiahbagh, *i.e.*, camel-coloured tiger.

The tiger was known to the ancients—he is the tigris Τίγρις of Latin and Greek authors. There is no doubt he figured in the Colosseum and other amphitheatres. Pliny, in his "Natural History," says, "The tiger is produced in Hyrcania and India;" and he alludes to its tremendous swiftness and fondness for its young. He says that Augustus was the first who showed a tigress in Rome, at the dedication of the Theatre of Marcellus; that the Emperor Claudius showed four tigers; and Suetonius speaks of tigers exhibited by Augustus. It was said by Dion that the Τίγρεις first seen by the Romans and Greeks were sent by the Indians, when they were sueing for peace from Augustus. The Emperor Philip, on one occasion, exhibited ten tigers, along with elephants, lions, and other wild beasts. Gordian, Antoninus, Elagabalus, and Aurelian also exhibited tigers, in the circensian games, or in triumphal processions.

Latin and Greek authors make frequent allusions to the tiger—Aristotle, Virgil, Horace, Martial, Claudian, Juvenal, Appian, and Pliny speak of him. In the Æneiad, Virgil makes Dido to say—

> "Duris genuit te Cautibus horrens,
> Caucasus, *Hyrcanæque* admôrunt ubera tigres."

Pictorial evidence is not wanting, were it necessary, to adduce additional proof that the true tiger was known in Rome; some mosaics found in that city exhibit the tiger (the real striped one) devouring his prey. They are thought to have been executed in commemoration of the exhibition by Claudius before mentioned. The tigers exhibited by the Romans were probably brought from the Elburz Mountains, south of the Caspian Sea—the ancient Hyrcania—and also from India; in these countries they still exist. But I believe tigers are seldom now seen on this side of the Indus.

Ancient accounts describe the tiger as being of tremendous strength, speed, and ferocity. Modern observers admit the strength and ferocity, as well as the agility with which it makes its bound or final rush on its prey, but deny its continued or sustained swiftness. In pursuit, or in a long run, it is soon overtaken and brought to bay. Indeed, it is the character of the felidæ generally to excel rather in bounds or sudden efforts of agility than in sustained speed, and the tiger is more remarkable in this respect, perhaps, than his congeners.

The tiger is a cat in all his actions, and those who have studied him in his native haunts must have been struck with their resemblance.

He is one of the symbols of power in the East; in China, the judicial throne is covered with his skin; and he has always occupied a prominent place in the menageries and parks, or rumnas, of Oriental princes, kept for show, and often, half or wholly tamed, led about by a chain, or confined in large cages and enclosures where he was made to fight with other tigers or with buffaloes, elephants, rhinoceros, or even with the horse and other animals, for the amusement of the native courts and their visitors.

I have seen several tiger fights at Lucknow in former years, before King Wajid Ally was deposed; and the memorable scene that followed that monarch's removal from his government—when an auction of tigers, leopards, cheetahs, elephants, rhinoceros, giraffes, and other animals, took place—had probably never been, and never will be, equalled. A dozen tigers, sold to the highest bidder, at ten rupees each, was perhaps one of the most remarkable purchases ever made, not surpassed even by that of a brace of rhinoceros at 250 rupees, or a giraffe at 500 rupees. All this has now changed; the rumnas and wild beasts have long since disappeared. Lucknow is no more as she has been. The tiger-throne of Hyder Ally, the tiger of Mysore, at Seringapatam, and his toy tiger devouring an English soldier, in which he is said to have delighted, are gone likewise. How different Hyder Ally and Tippoo Sultan must have been from the amiable and accomplished old gentleman, Tippoo's last surviving son, who died lately in Calcutta at a ripe old age! He was well known in England some years ago as Prince Gholam Mahomed, and was much respected by Europeans and natives in India.

The geographical distribution of the tiger is very wide. When Buffon stated that it was found, not only in Asia, but also in the South of Africa, he was mistaken, for it is confined entirely to the former country, though the area is a wide one. From Ararat and the Caucasus on the west, it ranges east as far as the Island of Saghalien, but it appears not to ascend to the high tableland of Thibet. From Cape Comorin it extends north in Hindostan to the Himalayas, to the height of 6,000 to 8,000 feet; one was killed recently, as reported in the *Home News* of February 2nd, 1874, at Dalhousie, 8,000 feet above the sea, the first, probably, that has been found so high.

Humboldt, in his "Central Asia," speaks of the tiger being found in Ceylon, but evidently he is mistaken. It is neither met with in that island nor in Borneo, notwithstanding that, with reference to the latter island, we find the following passage in Mr. St. John's work:—"At one place two rocks were pointed out to me in the stream, about thirty feet apart, called the Tiger's Leap. I made inquiries about these animals. They insist that eight came to their country (Borneo); that they were not tiger-cats, as I had suggested. If such animals were ever here, they might have escaped from cages in the capital, as it was a common custom among the far Eastern princes to keep these ferocious creatures, though I never heard of Bornean princes doing so. I have read somewhere that formerly there were a few tigers on the north-east coast, probably let loose by strangers, as the ancestors of the elephants were."*

It is found in Georgia, north of the Hindoo Koosh, in Bokhara, and Persia. South of the Caspian Sea; in the Elburz Mountains (the ancient Hyrcania), it is said to be numerous. On the shores of the Aral, Blyth says it proved troublesome to the Russian Surveying Expedition in the mid-winter, and it is found as far north as the shores of the Obi, and in the deserts which separate China from Siberia. It exists, according to A. Murray, "on the Irtisch, and in the Altai regions, and thence eastward to Amur-land, where it is very destructive to cattle; and so round by China, Siam, to all India southward of the Himalayas." Though absent from Ceylon and Borneo, it is found in Burmah and the Malayan peninsula as far south as Singapore, Java, Sumatra,

* St. John's "Life in the Forests of the Far East," vol. ii. p. 115.

THE GEOGRAPHICAL DISTRIBUTION OF THE TIGER.

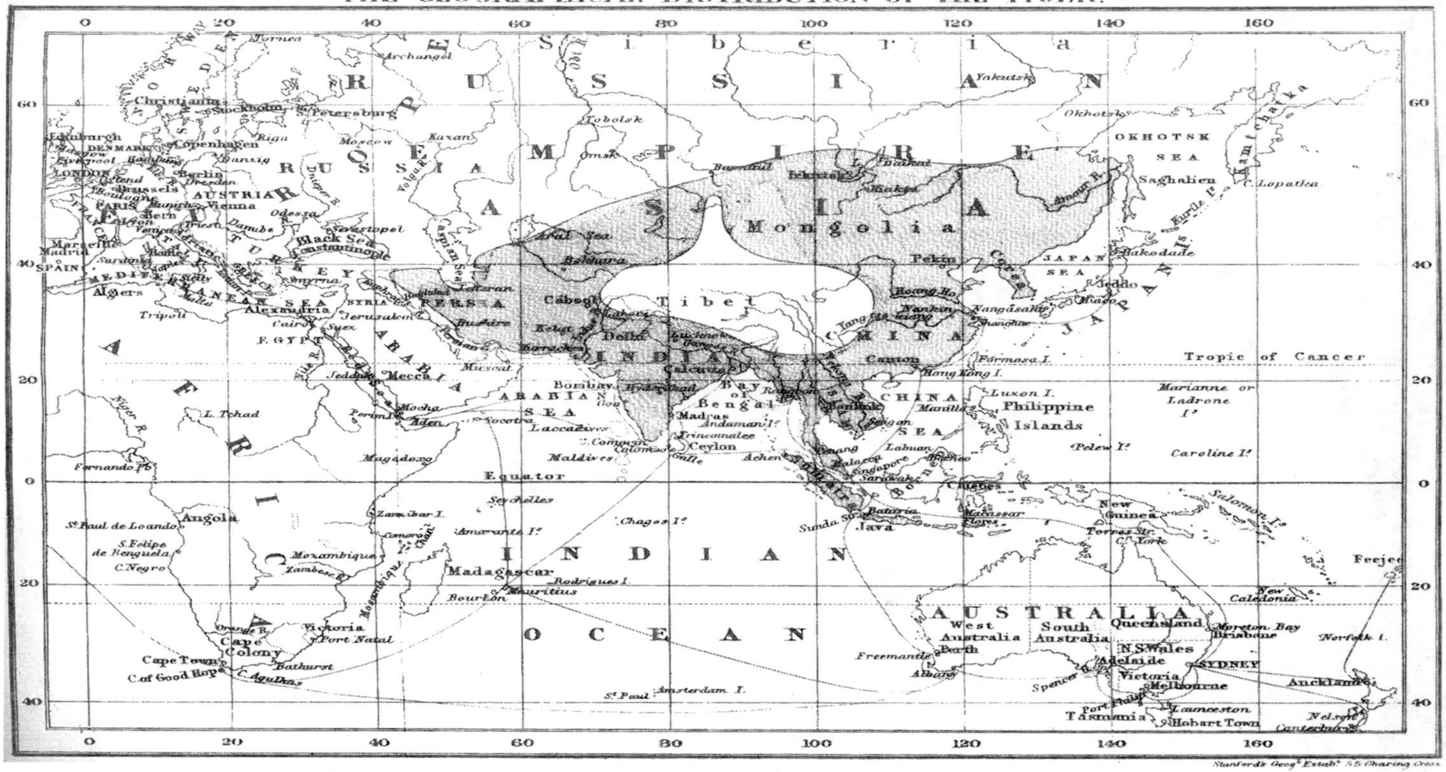

London: J & A. Churchill, New Burlington Street.

and perhaps in other islands of the Archipelago. Its extreme range is from 50° to 55° north on the confines of Siberia and China, to about 7° south in Java and the Indian Archipelago; from 143° east in the island of Saghalien, to about 40° west towards the shores of the Black Sea and the Caucasus. It is a mistake, therefore, to regard the tiger only as a tropical animal, though it is probable that the finest are found in the warm regions; and none are finer than those of Hindostan, and especially of Bengal.*

As has been said, there is only one species of tiger, (the clouded tiger, or Felis macrocelis, being a leopard), but no doubt he varies considerably in size, and depth or brilliancy of colouring, according to the climate, locality, and other circumstances. In the colder regions the hair is longer, thicker, and more fur like. My acquaintance with him has been chiefly in Bengal and the Terai, which may be regarded as his head-quarters in India; and amongst the finest specimens are those of Saugur Island and the Sunderbunds at the mouth of the Hooghly. Like cats, tigers attach themselves to certain localities, and a good tiger beat is sure to continue to be so

* Captain Lawson, in a recently published work, entitled "Wanderings in New Guinea," describes an animal very similar to the Bengal tiger, of which he shot three specimens in that island. It is to be hoped that Captain Lawson will publish a more detailed account of this tiger, and of its exact geographical position and range in New Guinea, where it has not hitherto been supposed to exist.

year after year. There are certain spots that are sure "finds," and you may rely on a tiger being there, though his predecessor may have been killed but recently, and such places or their vicinity are often selected as their nurseries. The long grass, especially the nul, is a favourite cover in which to deposit the cubs.

The tigress gives birth to from two to five, even six cubs. Three is a frequent number, and her period of gestation is said to be about fourteen to fifteen weeks. She is a most affectionate and attached mother, and generally guards and trains her young with the most watchful solicitude. They remain with her until nearly full grown, or about the second year, when they are able to kill for themselves, and begin life on their own account. Whilst they remain with her she is peculiarly vicious and aggressive, defending them with the greatest courage and energy, and when robbed of them is terrible in her rage, but she has been known to desert them when pressed, and even to eat them when starved. As soon as they begin to require other food than her milk, she kills for them, teaches them to do so for themselves by practising on small animals, such as deer and young calves or pigs. At these times she is wanton and extravagant in her cruelty, killing apparently for the gratification of her ferocious and blood-thirsty nature, and perhaps to excite and instruct the young ones, and it is not until they are thoroughly capable of killing their own food that she separates from them. The young tigers are far more destructive than the old. They will kill three or four cows at a time, whilst the older and more experienced rarely kill more than one, and this at intervals of from three or four days to a week. For this purpose the tiger will leave its retreat in the dense jungle, proceed to the neighbourhood of a village or gowrie, where cattle feed, and during the night will steal on and strike down a bullock, drag it into a secluded place, and then remain near the "murrie" or "kill" for several days, until it has eaten it, when it will proceed in search of a further supply, and having found good hunting ground in the vicinity of a village or gowrie, continue its ravages, destroying one or two cows or buffaloes a week. It is very fond of the ordinary domestic cattle which, in the plains of India, are generally weak, half-starved, under-sized creatures. One of these is easily struck down and carried or dragged off. The smaller buffaloes are also easily disposed of, but the buffalo bulls, and especially the wild ones, are formidable antagonists, and have often been known to beat the tiger off, and even to wound him seriously with their horns.

Cattle and buffaloes especially, seem to have an instinctive knowledge of the proximity of a tiger, probably from the scent, and one may generally guess that a tiger is present in a swampy patch of long grass if the cattle refuse to enter it, which they would otherwise be only too glad to do, for the sake of the fresh and succulent grass that they find there. The attack of the tiger is generally, though not always, made in the night. He watches the cattle, creeps stealthily out until within springing or rather rushing distance, then, with a rush or bound and a roar or deep growl, he seizes it by the throat and drags or strikes it to the ground with his formidable arm, fixes his fangs in the throat, his powerful fore claws in the trunk or neck, and holds it there until it is nearly or quite dead, when he drags it off to the jungle to be devoured at leisure. The first morsels are generally torn from the flank or hind quarter. Near the "kill" is the lair or "beithuck," a space where the grass is trodden down something like a hare's form. From this he proceeds as his appetite prompts him to the "kill," until it is eaten and even the bones gnawed, by which time, owing to the heat of the weather, it is far advanced in decomposition, and the "kill" is revealed, not only by the odour, but by the flocks of vultures, kites, crows, and adjutants wheeling and soaring in the air above it, and by prowling jackals. The vultures also sit with a gorged and sleepy aspect in the branches of the surrounding trees, from which they descend from time to time to make a meal when the tiger has left it, or even to snatch a morsel whilst he is feeding, and often disputing its possession with him, a temerity for which they sometimes pay with their lives from a sudden stroke of his fore paw.

When gorged with his first meal, the tiger is sluggish and drowsy. He dislikes being disturbed, and is not easily roused; in this state, being far less formidable and indisposed to fight than a lean and hungry tigress, who has her young ones to defend and care for, he is frequently surprised and slain. He feeds on cattle when he can get them, for they are easily killed, and furnish an ample meal, but as they are not always forthcoming, he has often to seek his food elsewhere. In India the hog deer (Cervus porcinus), the cheetul or spotted deer (Cervus axis), the karker (Cervus muntjac) or barking deer, the sambur (Rusa aristotelii), the gôen or swamp deer (Rucervus duvaucelii), the nil-ghye (Portax picta), the wild hog, occasionally monkeys, even pea-fowl, and other smaller animals, become his prey. The pig is said to be an especial favourite, though it sometimes happens that in attempting to kill a boar he meets with more than his match, and is beaten off and even mortally wounded by its tusks. When the buffaloes know, as they often seem to do, that a tiger is near them, they form into a circle or phalanx, the males on the outside, where they face about to receive him. Under these circumstances the attack is generally deferred until some weak member of the herd is caught incautiously straggling from the rest, and is then struck down; not unfrequently, even then, they charge the tiger, drive him off, and rescue their wounded comrade. I have seen young buffaloes that had been thus recovered, and though lame and sickly looking, they were not always mortally injured. The approach of a tiger is often revealed to the herdsman by the deportment of the buffaloes: they form into a circle, within which he finds safety in retiring, a proceeding which is evidently comprehended and encouraged by the buffaloes themselves. In times of want, when other food is scarce, tigers have been known to eat each other, or, it is said, carrion not killed by themselves. Frogs and other small animals are not despised, and even the porcupine sometimes become their prey. A case is recorded where a tiger was killed, in an extreme state of emaciation, with a quill sticking in his gullet, which had become impacted there when eating the porcupine. The tiger, and the tigress too, sometimes eat their own young, and when she brings forth in captivity, it is said, she requires to be more than usually well fed to prevent her from devouring her offspring.

The tiger is a shy, morose, unsociable brute, and is often found quite alone, though at certain seasons his mate, if not present, is probably not far away. Four or even five tigers have been seen basking in the sun together in ruins like those of Gour, but the party generally consists of the members of a nearly full-grown family, and though the young ones are still with their mother, they are probably about to leave her and start in life on their own account. A tigress, whose skin now before me measures 9 feet 4 inches from snout to tip of tail, with her three full-grown cubs, all fell together within a circle of 100 yards in diameter, in the Nepal Terai, one evening in the end of April, 1871, on the last occasion when the best of viceroys and the keenest of sportsmen was the life and soul of a party who swept those noted tiger beats, little anticipating the great calamity that was so soon to deprive them of their much loved leader.

The tiger is found in most of the tree and grass jungles throughout India. Those more remote from population and cultivation are more frequented, though when compelled by hunger he visits and even takes up his abode in the vicinity of the more open, cultivated parts, and in so doing becomes the dread and pest of the villagers, who are in constant apprehension for their own or for the lives of their cattle, though in justice we must say more frequently the latter than the former. During the cold and rainy seasons he is a peripatetic creature, restless and wandering from place to place. At these seasons he probably has no fixed abode, though he keeps within a certain range of country. When the tree or grass jungle is thick, and gives general cover or shelter, he roams freely from place to place, seeking what he may devour, and during these seasons is safer from his human enemies than in the months of March, April, and May, which, in Bengal, Oude, and the North of India generally, is the tiger-hunting season. During these months the extensive plains of long grass and much of the underwood and scrub disappear. They are burned, in fact, to promote the growth of the next year's crop, and thus, what was formerly a dense and endless cover, now becomes an open plain or cleared out forest. The heat too becomes intense. At these seasons the tigers are found in patches of long grass, the nurkool or nul, which are kept fresh and green by pools of water or swamps. Here, and in the edges of the forest, they lie at rest during the heat of the day, sheltered from the rays of the sun by the tall reed-like grass, which is from twenty to thirty feet high, and cooled by the moisture. These swamps, or baghars, as they are called in Oude, are often treacherously deep, and are dangerous to the elephants from the phussun or quagmire so often found there. These grassy retreats occur on the outskirts of the forest, frequently near villages or gowries (cow-feeding stations), and the tigers inhabiting them become the pest and scourge of the place, for though shy and solitary they must have food, and will come where it is most easily obtained, and their wants are not supplied by less than an average of about a cow every third day; in some cases where he has fallen into evil ways, and has found out that it is easy and pleasant to kill a man, he causes great destruction of human life, and he will soon depopulate a village by killing some, and frightening away the rest of the inhabitants. He is not by any means confined to these grassy plains or swamps, but is found also in the forests, and indeed wherever the necessary shelter, food, and water exist.

Sometimes he affects ruins, and those of the ancient city of Gour, where lie imbedded the débris of former stately buildings, among dense jungle of corunda (Zyziphus jujuba), are a favourite resort. The patches of tamarisk by the river sides or on the churs (sandbanks), the grass, rattan, and other underwood in many places, abound with tigers; the rocky ravines and scrub-covered hill sides and nullahs also give them shelter, and are chiefly the characteristics of the habitat of the tiger in the Bombay and Madras Presidencies, which make tiger shooting so different there, to what it is in Bengal.

It is generally admitted that the tiger attains the greatest size in India, and there can be no doubt that he is really the largest of the existing felidæ. Blyth says that he believes that the largest tigers considerably exceed in size the largest lions. Radde says he has compared skulls from the Amour, from Caucasus, and India, and that he found the latter considerably larger than the others. The Caucasian tiger appears to be remarkable for the small size of the upper canines. The size of the tiger varies; some individuals attain great bulk and weight, though they are shorter than others which are of a slighter and more elongated form. The statements as to the length they attain are conflicting and often exaggerated; errors are apt to arise from measurements taken from the skin after it is stretched, when it may be ten or twelve inches longer than before removal from the body. The tiger should be measured from the nose along the spine to the tip of the tail as he lies dead on the spot where he fell before the skin is removed. One that is ten feet by this measurement is large, and the full-grown male does not often exceed this, though no doubt larger individuals (males) are occasionally seen, and I have been informed by Indian sportsmen of reliability, that they have seen and killed tigers over 12 feet in length. The full-grown male Indian tiger therefore may be said to be from 9 to 12 feet or 12 feet 2 inches, the tigress from 8 to 10, or perhaps, in very rare instances, 11 feet in length, the height being from 3 to 3½, or, very rarely, 4 feet at the shoulder.

But we must look with doubt on Buffon's statement that one had attained the length of 15 feet; and with even greater hesitation can we accept the recorded statement that Hyder Ally presented a tiger to the Nawab of Arcot that measured 18 feet.

Wherever the tiger is found he roams undisputed master of the locality, and the destruction of life he causes is often great. His favourite food, as I have said, is cattle, deer, and the wild hog; and, according to some, the pea-fowl; and it is a remarkable fact that wherever he is found these birds may be looked for too; though it is probable that this is due rather to the nature of the cover than to any preference for pea-fowl. I remember, in a shooting expedition in the Nepal Terai, with the Nepalese minister, Jung Bahadur, who was accompanied by about 400 elephants, to have seen, when the tiger was surrounded in long grass and low scrubby jungle, that as the circle of elephants gradually closed in, numerous pea-fowl were enclosed also, and became so frightened by the towering wall of howdahs, that some were picked up by the piadehs, or foot-men accompanying the elephants, being too frightened and confused to rise from the long grass and fly over and beyond the mighty circle by which they were hemmed in. In such grassy places a tiger, with his silent and stealthy tread, would easily approach, and might seize the birds before they could disentangle themselves and escape out of the long grass. It is said that the tiger sometimes attacks the alligators, or gurriáls, as they lie basking on the banks of the rivers, or on sand-banks, the margins of which are often fringed with the tamarisk, long grass, or other congenial cover. This may be possible when other food has failed, and it is said that it occasionally happens that he falls a victim in the attempt, more than one instance being recorded of his having been seized by the powerful jaws of the alligator, dragged into the river, and drowned. There is a fine illustration of a tiger being so treated by a large alligator, in a picture by Wolf, recently published. As the tiger is found on the margins of swamps and rivers which teem with these great saurians, it is possible that such an incident may occasionally occur, though I confess I feel inclined to relegate it to the category of travellers' stories. It is said also that he is sometimes surprised and destroyed by the great python (P. mollurus) of the Indian jungle and swamps; and though I have no knowledge of, or scarcely any belief in such an occurrence, I think it not absolutely impossible; for I have seen and helped to kill a python nearly twenty feet in length, which probably would have been equal to the destruction of a tiger, had it been so inclined, and had the opportunity occurred. There can be no doubt that the destruction of human beings by tigers is very great in India (though the actual amount may have been exaggerated), as well as in other localities where they abound—and where they become man-eaters, the sacrifice of life is often serious. It is said that these man-eaters are generally, though not always, very old tigers, whose teeth have become blunted or defective.

The tiger is generally most dangerous to cattle, but not always so. In some parts of India the man-eater appears to be the rule rather than the exception. Jerdon says that in Central India, in the Mudlah district, near Jubbulpore, in 1856 and previous years, an average of between 200 and 300 villagers were killed yearly by tigers. Captain B. Rogers, Bengal army, has lately drawn a melancholy picture of the ravages committed on human beings; and only lately I observe that Government has appointed an officer in the Madras Presidency especially for the purpose of destroying tigers. It is said that when a tiger has once killed a man, and tasted human flesh, he prefers it to all other food. Whether this be true or not I cannot say; but there can be no doubt that when once the dread, natural in all animals, of the human form has been overcome, the man-eater becomes so formidable as sometimes to cause the depopulation of a village and become the dread of a district. That this is not always the character of the tiger is proved by the indifference with which he is often regarded by the natives, who carry on their usual avocations as herdsmen, cultivators, wood and grass cutters, close to the cover in which they know he is concealed. This may arise either from their peculiarly apathetic or fatalistic character, or from the experience which teaches them that, generally, so long as the tiger is unmolested, and has other food, he will not injure men. But it is not less certain that over many roads and along many paths through the forest or grass, men will not pass at night, or even in the day, alone, without torches or tomtoms to scare away the enemy that they believe is lurking ready to seize them as they pass. It sometimes happens that a road or path is closed for weeks or months by a tiger, and only becomes safe after some European or native shikari has met and destroyed the enemy. Not only postmen, herdsmen, and casual foot travellers are occasionally seized and carried off, but even those travelling on horseback or in hackeries (bullock carts) have been taken. Yet, withal, it is strange to see the apparent indifference with which the cowherds and villagers often regard the formidable brute. Cow after cow is attacked and killed, or occasionally recovered by the herdsmen, who frighten the tiger off the body of the stricken creature, by shouting or beating their sticks on the ground; and over and over again I have been taken by these aheers (herdsmen) up to the "kill" on foot (for they will often refuse to mount an elephant), without the slightest evidence of fear, and when the tiger is on foot, or perhaps wounded and ready to charge, they will stand near or form a line, and beat him out of the jungle. Should he pass near one of them he is pretty certain to strike him down, perhaps inflict a dangerous wound, either with claws or teeth; but he is much less likely to do this if unwounded.

Dr. J. Anderson, in his Western Yunan Expedition, narrates the following incident, in reference to a man-eater:—"While we were at dinner one evening in Bhamo, a cry was raised that a tiger was in the town, and we at once started with our rifles, and were met by a man who informed us that a woman had been killed; we hurried on, and in a hollow, before a clump of bamboos, came upon the body of the poor woman, over which her niece was crying bitterly. The back of the skull was completely smashed in, and part of the scalp was torn off. The woman had been sitting in the low verandah of a ground hut, making thatch, and had evidently been whisked off by one fell swoop of the tiger's paw, for no marks of the teeth could be discovered. A number of people were seated close beside her, talking loudly; but this only verifies what I have heard about man-eating tigers, that they rather take advantage than otherwise of a noise to secure their prey; and this one, a tigress, had a decided partiality for human flesh, for she had carried off another woman a year before, and the townspeople attested that she cleared the stockade, nine feet high, with the woman in her mouth. In the present instance she had dragged her prey about fifty yards, but whenever the people discovered what had happened they rushed from their houses with torches, and shouting drove her off. When we arrived there were fifty men, all armed with spears and guns, and many carried torches, and fires had been lit in every direction, to frighten the brute away. The scene was a most exciting and effective picture; we had the body removed, and beat the thickets, but could discover no trace of the tigress. The woman was buried the same night, in accordance with the Burmese custom, followed in all cases of persons killed by tigers. On the following morning we found the tracks of the animal clearly imprinted on fresh bricks laid out to dry, and its sex indicated by the footprints of her cub."

The Rev. Mr. Mason, in his work on "Tenasserim,"

says, "Twice during my residence in Tavoy they (tigers) came into the gate of my compound, broke open the door of the goat-house, and succeeded in killing a goat each time before they could be routed. On another occasion, while sleeping in a jungle-hamlet, a tiger leaped into a buffalo-pen close by the house and killed a buffalo. They appear to be afraid to encounter man until they have once had a contest with him, when all fear ceases ever after. I have encamped in the jungles often where the tracks of tigers were seen all around in the morning within a few yards of where myself and people had bivouacked; yet they never ventured an attack. But whenever a tiger has once tasted human blood, it even seeks it in preference to all others. A Burman was struck down by a tiger at the head of Tavoy river, and he was seen by his companions to inflict a severe wound on his antagonist with his knife, but was carried off. A few months afterwards a karen was killed by a tiger in a village twenty miles distant, and when the villagers subsequently succeeded in killing the animal, it was found to have been wounded as described by the Burmans. A karen was killed by a tiger near a village a dozen miles east of Tavoy, supposed to be the same beast that had devoured a man ten miles distant a short time previous. This karen was carried off after breakfast in the morning while going out alone to his work in the field, and no less than a week from that time a Burman was struck down by a tiger in the middle of the day, not six miles distant, and when there were eight other men in company.

"A karen who was killed by a tiger near the forks of the Tenasserim, was walking with three others in company a couple of hours before sunset, and had a gun on his shoulder. The karens that lived nearest immediately set traps in the paths that led to their villages, and the animal was soon caught near one of their houses.

"On one occasion I reached a lone karen village at dusk, and was surprised to find it barricaded all round to prevent access. On inquiry, I found that two men had been devoured by a tiger the day before in the neighbourhood close by. It appeared that one man had been carried off, and four others armed themselves and went in pursuit; after a day's search, and while in the track, the beast came out boldly on the plain and succeeded in carrying off one of the armed karens who had engaged in the pursuit.

"A few years ago a little body of karens removed from Yay and settled on the upper part of Tavoy river; but, after losing four or five men in as many different years by the tigers, they have been compelled to descend into the more populous parts of the valley."

The natives of India, especially the Hindoos, hold the tiger, as they do the cobra, in superstitious awe.

Many would not kill him if they could, for they fear that he will haunt them or do them mischief after death. Some they regard as being the tenement of a spirit, which not only renders them immortal, but confers increased powers of mischief. In many parts of India the peasants will hardly mention the tiger by name. They either call him, as in Purneah, gidhur (jackal), janwar (the beast), or they will not name him at all; and it is the same in the case of the wolf. But though they will not always themselves destroy him, they are quite willing that others should do so, for they will point out his whereabouts and be present at his death; and the delight evinced thereat is intense, for it often relieves a whole village from an incubus of no slight weight, and saves the herdsman from his weekly loss of cattle. The conversation and remarks made by these villagers round the fallen tiger are often very amusing and characteristic.

All kinds of power and influence are ascribed to portions of him when dead; the fangs, the claws, the whiskers, are potent charms, medicines, love-philters, or prophylactics against disease, the evil eye, or magic. They are in such demand that the natives *will* take them; and we have known whiskers, claws, and even fangs extracted or carried away during the night, even when the dead tiger has been placed under the surveillance of a guard. The fat, also, is in great demand for its many potent virtues in relieving rheumatism and other ailments. The liver, the heart, and the flesh are taken away and dried, to be eaten as tonics or invigorating remedies that give strength and courage. There is also a popular delusion that a new lobe is added to the liver every year of his life. A tiger-skin with its whiskers preserved is a rarity; you cannot keep them. The domestic, who would preserve any other valuable as a most sacred trust, will fail under this temptation! The whiskers, besides other wonderful powers, are said to possess that of being a slow poison when administered with the food; such is the belief, which you may try in vain to disturb! The clavicles, too, little curved bones like tiny ribs, are also much valued; but they are generally lost or overlooked when the tiger is cut up, lying buried in the powerful muscles near the shoulder.

Captain B. Rogers, of the Indian army, who has studied the habits of the wild animals of India, recently read a remarkable and interesting paper on the subject of the ravages committed by them, before the Society of Arts, in London, and gave, with other important information, details, of which I have extracted some items, as illustrative of the magnitude of the evil.

Captain R., who is an experienced sportsman, has suggested a comprehensive scheme for the destruction of wild beasts, which, no doubt, if carried out, would somewhat diminish the evil. A model of a trap invented by him for the destruction of tigers was exhibited in the South Kensington Museum.

Speaking of the destruction of life by wild animals, Captain R. says, in Lower Bengal alone, in a period of six years ending in 1866, 13,400 human beings were killed by wild animals, whilst 18,196 wild animals were killed in the same period at a cost of 65,000 rupees; and it appears, moreover, that the Government reports show that in these six years ending in 1866, 4,218 persons were killed by tigers, 1,407 by leopards, 4,287 by wolves, and the remainder by other animals; the tiger and wolf thus claiming nearly equal shares. The worst district in Bengal Proper is that of Rungpore, in the Rajshahye Division, the yearly loss of life being between 55 and 60 persons. In Bengal Proper alone about 1,200 tigers are killed annually; of these 4 per cent. are cubs. Next to Bengal come the Central Provinces, and then certain parts of Madras.

The Chief Commissioner's reports of the Central Provinces show that in 1866–67, 372; in 1867–68, 289; in 1868–69, 285 persons were killed by tigers.

The District Magistrate from Dhera Dhoon writes:—"Man-eating tigers are quite an exception in Oude and Rohilcund; one is heard of in every six years, but he is invariably killed after a short lapse of time." Captain Rogers says, however, that tigers are man-eaters by nature and instinct, not by education; "men, therefore, are liable to be eaten where tigers exist."

One gentleman, writing from Nayadunka in July, 1869, says—"Cattle killed in my district are numberless. As regards human beings, one tiger in 1867–1868–1869 killed respectively 27, 34, 47 people. I have known it attack a party, and kill four or five at a time. Once it killed a father, mother, and three children; and the week before it was shot it killed seven people. It wandered over a tract of twenty miles, never remaining in the same spot two consecutive days, and at last was destroyed by a bullet from a spring gun when returning to feed at the body of one of its victims—a woman.

"At Nynee Tal in Kumaon, in 1856–57–58, there was a tiger that prowled about within a circle say of twenty miles, and it killed on an average about eighty men per annum. The haunts were well known at all seasons. * * * * This tiger was afterwards shot while devouring the body of an aged person it had killed."

Captain R. relates an incident which illustrates the superstition of the native in regard to tigers:—

"A tiger in Chota Nagpore destroyed a great number of lives. * * * * I had a weapon set across its known path, and it was only a matter of hours before his career was stopped. But what was the result? Numbers of the natives in the vicinity, including those I had employed to set the trap, ran off when they heard of the animal's death, and did not return for days, as they felt sure that when dead it would be revenged on them, and take the form of a human corpse so as to get them hanged for murder. The remains were not, on that account, shown to me until decomposed." Further, he remarks, "When a Ghônd or Kurkoo (the people inhabiting certain wild tracts) is killed by a tiger, the wife, children, and parents are thrown out of caste—all intercourse between them and other inhabitants being interdicted, on the ground that they are labouring under the displeasure of the Deity. In fact, the man-eating tiger is the deity to whom those wild and ignorant aborigines offer prescribed sacrifices on the occasion of their having suffered from its ravages; thus the injury they have incurred is increased, and the previously scanty means of these helpless creatures are doubly taxed."

Again, quoting a Government report—"In one instance, in the Central Provinces, a single tigress caused the desertion of thirteen villages, and two hundred and fifty square miles of country were thrown out of cultivation. This state of things would undoubtedly have continued, but for the timely arrival of a gentleman who happily was fortunate enough, with the aid of his gun, to put an end to her eventful career."

In 1868 the Magistrate of Godavery reported "that part of the country was over-run with tigers, every village having suffered from the ravages of man-eaters. No road was safe, and a few days before his arrival at Kondola, a tiger charged a large body of villagers within a few hundred yards of the civil station."

Again, it is reported that one tigress, in 1869, killed 127 people, and stopped a public road for many weeks, and was finally killed by the opportune arrival of an English sportsman."

Other instances might be added, but the above are sufficient to prove how fierce and destructive tigers can be, not only to cattle and other lower animals, but to human beings.

We are startled by its magnitude, when we read Captain Rogers' statement "that the loss of property which the ravages of the carnivora entailed amounted annually to ten million pounds." Great it no doubt is, but we would hope that Captain R. has over-estimated the amount. It would be interesting to know how much—a large share no doubt—is attributable to tigers alone.

The tiger likes to be at rest in his cover, to bask in the sun, or recline in the shade, according to the weather; in the great heats, when he is most readily found and shot, he likes the cool wet grass, and will often take to the water. He loves to select the vicinity of good food and water, and to remain there for a season, until changing circumstances prompt removal elsewhere. The full-grown tiger is not wantonly destructive: he kills only to eat; and when he is not hungry, unless provoked, animals about him are safe, and he will remain near, or pass close to men and cattle without molesting them. It is not so, as I have said, with the younger tigers, or with the tigress when training her young. They kill for mere sport. The confirmed man-eaters, preferring human flesh, establish themselves where it is most easily procured, and become more cunning, wary, and stealthy than others; it is said they are generally old animals. The tiger seems to be particular about the state of his claws, they are always kept sharp, polished, carefully protected within the sheath of integument, and are kept from contact with the ground, and thus remain pointed and clean, being very formidable weapons, with which fearful wounds are inflicted. Probably it is to keep them in order, clean and bright, that the tiger is so fond of scratching the bark of trees; and the deep vertical scorings, up to a height of ten or twelve feet, are often seen on the Indian fig or other tree. They have favourites which they select or set apart for this purpose, and the scorings are very deep and numerous. I remember a

Ficus venosa by the side of a nul-swamp in Purneah, under whose shade I have often rested in the middle of a hot day's tiger shooting in March or April. It stood alone, and was evidently a favourite resort of the tigers, for it was deeply and numerously scored by their claws.

Tigers do not, as a general rule, climb trees; but when pressed by fear, as during an inundation, or when no other way of escape offers from real or imaginary danger, they have occasionally been known to do so. They have also been seen to clamber up or even spring to a certain height, where they have seen a man, and whence they thought the shot came, and pull him down. I have heard of authentic instances where this happened. Nor are they wont to spring to any great height from the ground; though an instance occurred recently, related by an eye-witness, where a tiger pulled a native, in one spring, out of a tree at a height of eighteen feet from the ground. The tiger's usual attack is a rush accompanied by a series of short deep growls or roars, in which he evidently thinks he will do much by intimidation; when he charges home he rises on the hind feet, seizes with the teeth and claws, endeavours, and often succeeds, in pulling down the object seized. They do occasionally leave the ground with a spring, clear a fence or ditch, or even alight on the elephant's head, his pad, or hind quarters; but this probably happens in the case of tigresses or young and active males. The heavy old tiger seldom, if ever, is so energetic in springing up heights; though he will take a good broad ditch or wall, etc., in a bound.

I have been told by an eye-witness of an incident that illustrates not only the tiger's activity but his strength when he chooses to exert them. A tiger at a bound sprang from an elevation right among a herd of cattle, and in his spring struck down simultaneously a cow with each fore foot. Both were disabled; one, he immediately killed and began to devour, whilst the other wretched creature lay with its back broken by the tiger's terrible blow within a few feet watching the fate of its companion. In this position the group was seen by my informant, who added that he never saw such an expression of terror and suffering as was depicted by the wretched cow. The tiger unfortunately escaped. It must be remembered that when a tiger stands on his hind feet, his fore paws reach nine to twelve feet high, and this brings him well up to the head, hind quarters, or pad of an elephant. Having seized, he holds tenaciously, and if he makes a good grip with his hind claws he may get higher. The fore claws are driven fiercely in, and elephants are often severely lacerated by them. On one occasion I remember to have seen a tigress pull a large elephant down till her head almost rested on the ground, simply from the intense pain caused by the implanted claws. The tigress was partly shaken, partly shot off the elephant's head, and killed. In the evening, when the elephant was being attended to, and having her scratches washed and dressed, the mahout called my attention to a claw that had been wrenched from the tigress's foot and remained deeply imbedded in the elephant's head above the eye. It is a popular belief, and by no means confined to the ignorant, that the wounds inflicted by the fangs and claws of the tiger are very dangerous and of a specific nature. This, however, is a mistake. It is certainly possible that the teeth and claws may occasionally be contaminated with septic matters from the decomposing flesh of his prey; but this is probably rare, as any one would say who saw these weapons and know the careful way in which they are kept polished and clean. The fact is, the wounds owe their dangerous condition to the fact of their being deeply punctured or lacerated; otherwise they have no peculiarity, and they not unfrequently heal very readily, though they are occasionally followed by profuse suppuration, which as in similar wounds may induce blood poisoning. I have seen the severest injuries inflicted by the tiger recovered from rapidly, others after profuse suppuration and sloughing of the torn and stretched tissues.

It is remarkable how many people escape who have been wounded by tigers. They seldom kill on the spot, and, unless in the case of the man-eater, rarely take the human victim far, if at all, from the spot where he is struck down. The action is generally a bite about the shoulder or head, a shake or two, perhaps he drags the victim for a few paces and then drops and leaves him, having crushed the shoulder or limb, or deeply wounded the scalp or neck, in some instances having fractured the skull and thus caused death, or he gives a blow of the paw and a shake or two, and then leaves him. This is generally the case when the tiger is alarmed or when he is encountered suddenly and thinks he is in danger; if not molested, and if he see his way to escape, he, as a general rule, will turn out of the way into the nearest cover with a menacing growl, but without attacking. Several instances are on record where the victim was seized, carried off, but ultimately dropped, and made his escape; a friend, since dead, was thus seized and dragged many yards by a tiger, but was relinquished, and without any very serious injury. Where a man is taken for food he is carried off and eaten as a deer would be; though even in such cases escapes have been effected.

The tiger takes the water readily and is a good swimmer. The Saugur Island and Soonderbund tigers continually swim from one island to the other, to change their hunting grounds for deer. They have more than once been surprised by the river steamers, or by boats, and killed in the water. It is said that they swim from Singapore to the neighbouring islands. They will, when hunted, or even in the usual course of their travels, swim across large pools in the forest, or in the swamps, or even rivers. It is not many years since one got on board a Soonderbund steamer, when lying at anchor, and for a time took possession of the deck, and was at last shot by the captain. They frequently cross the Ganges, and I have traced them by their footprints

FIG. 4

TIGER'S FORE-FOOTPRINT.

to the water's edge on one bank and taken up the track again on the other side. (*See* Fig.) Though a tiger seldom does so, he can spring to a considerable height if he likes. A friend, one of the most experienced tiger shots in India, relates an instance where a tigress having been fired at from a tree, or some other concealed place, sprang into a machàn in a field, at least ten or twelve feet from the ground, thinking the shot came from there, and by her weight and the force of her spring brought it all to the ground; it was empty, the shot had not come thence.

A machàn is a platform erected on a frame, or in

a tree, from which a herdsman watches cattle or the grain, or the sportsman waits for game; it is often used for shooting from, and sometimes is erected in a tree for the purpose of tiger shooting, when the jungle is beaten and the game driven towards it.

Tigers have occasionally but very rarely been shot in trees. As they are not tree climbers, the occasions on which they would be found there are quite exceptional; I have already alluded to this, and to their fondness for scratching the bark of trees with their claws.

Though preferring the solitudes of his jungle cover, he occasionally finds his way into a village, sometimes even into the villagers' huts. This only happens when impelled by hunger and attracted by food, in which case, being near a village, he may have endeavoured, in his anxiety to take advantage of the first cover, to conceal himself there. I have known a tiger to be killed in the underwood, in a tope of trees, quite close to a village. This tiger had no doubt often roamed through, or close to the village in the night. Sportsmen have often heard them near their tents at night. The roar of the tiger as conventionally understood, is seldom heard; he generally makes a few short grunts or barks, or savage growls, when roused, attacked, or wounded, and when he charges. During the stillness of the night, which is only disturbed by the gentle murmur of a mountain rapid, or the sighing of the wind through the branches of the Seesoo forest, all camp sounds being hushed, the prolonged deep wailing howl of the tiger and tigress calling to each other is often heard, and an imposing sound it is, making one feel glad not to be alone or abroad in the forest, and to have the shelter of a tent and the feeling of security given by the belongings of the camp around one. The nocturnal proceedings of the tiger are, no doubt, very cat-like ; only on a grander scale.

It seems to be the impression that tigers have not diminished much, if at all, in numbers in India, since 1857. In certain localities where cultivation and population have extended, where jungle has been cleared away, and land reclaimed from the forest or the swamp, they have thinned or disappeared ; but such conditions are rare in comparison with the large uncultivated areas over which the tiger still roams ; indeed, in those outlying places on the edge of the forest and in belts of jungle, where cattle grazing is the occupation of the sparsely-scattered population, it is probable that the tiger has increased rather than diminished of late years, in consequence of the general disarming of the people, which became necessary after the Mutiny of 1857. The subject has attracted the consideration of Government both at home and in India, and it is to be hoped that more decided measures than any hitherto taken, will be the result of the interest this undoubtedly important subject has excited. A more systematic method of dealing with the evil may be needed, and some general and combined action on the part of the authorities, but it must not be supposed that nothing has been done. A system of rewards has long existed, and the sums paid for tigers, leopards, wolves, form a large item in the yearly accounts of most district officers in India. The reward paid by Government for the destruction of tigers is generally, I believe, at the rate of ten rupees a head; in the case of a notorious man-eater, more is given. Within the last year an officer has been appointed in the Madras Presidency whose duty it is to destroy tigers and other wild beasts, and this is perhaps a preliminary to other arrangements on the part of Government for a similar object.

The methods of destroying tigers are numerous. They are snared in pit-falls and traps, shot by spring guns, and arrows, occasionally poisoned, and it is said that bird-lime has been used in their destruction. I have read of this, but know of no authenticated case in which it has been practised. The bird-lime, it is said, is spread on the fallen leaves ; these adhering to the tiger's paws are soon plastered all over him, including his face and eyes. Blinded and stupefied by rage and fear, he falls an easy prey to the villagers, who then either shoot or stab him to death with spears. We read in Allen's *Indian Mail* of February 24th, 1874: "It would almost seem as if the tiger, in fear of strychnine, toda-traps, and Captain Caulfield's guns, had resolved to retire to the Hills. We lately mentioned the fact of four tigers having been seen in company not far from Ooty.

We have since heard that a native bringing toddy from the plains to the bakery at Conoor, was seized somewhere in the Conoor Ghat, and carried off by a tiger."

One mode of effecting his death is to lay a bait by tying up a cow or goat in some spot the tiger is wont to frequent; near this, on a machàn or on the branch of a tree or from behind some extemporised screen, the shikarie waits his approach at night, and when the bait is seized takes aim, and often succeeds in destroying him, though it not unfrequently happens that in the uncertain light he misses altogether or only wounds, in which case a second chance is seldom obtained. It sometimes happens that the sportsman, tired by waiting and watching, falls asleep, and awakes only to see the prey carried off, and too late to get an effective shot. Many tigers are thus yearly destroyed, but still numbers remain, and the destruction of life and property caused by them goes on, though I am inclined to think not to so great an extent as is sometimes represented; and when it is borne in mind that the population of India, including the Native States, is nearly 250,000,000, the proportion of deaths is not so large as it at first sight seems to be, and probably would not contrast so very unfavourably with mortality from what should be preventible causes at home—railway accidents, for example! Far be it from me to suggest ought that might appear to involve danger to human life, but I must say that I should regard the complete extinction of tigers with a regret something akin to that with which annihilation of the fox would be regarded in England. So far as the sportsmen and their followers are concerned, serious and fatal accidents are not more frequent from the claws and teeth of tigers than they are in fox-hunting in England, from falls and the chances of the field.

I certainly would not preserve tigers, and would encourage their destruction, but by hunting, rather than by poison* or the snare. Of course, when no sportsmen are at hand, they should be destroyed without law, when and where they could be found.

There are several ways of compassing the tiger's death resorted to by sportsmen, and they are practised according to circumstances, the nature of the country, and the opportunities at command. In Bengal, Central India, the North West, and the Terai, where he is found chiefly in jungle and grass or swamps, and where he would generally be perfectly inaccessible on foot, the tiger is hunted from elephants, and there certainly is no more exciting or nobler sport; or he is driven in a hunqua (a drive) from his forest or grassy retreat, towards trees or other elevated spots, in which machàns are placed, from which the sportsman aims in tolerable safety,

* Poisoning by strychnine has recently been resorted to in the Madras Presidency, where an officer has been appointed by Government to compass the destruction of tigers.

and often succeeds in securing his game. In Madras, Bombay, some parts of Bengal, Central India, and the Central Provinces, the tiger is often hunted on foot, and it is in this dangerous sport that fatal and serious accidents are liable to happen, for no accuracy of aim or steadiness of nerve can always guard against or prevent the rush of even a mortally wounded tiger, that in his very death-throes may inflict a dangerous or fatal injury. I have known more than one such case, and too many have occurred. This exciting and dangerous sport is sometimes, from the nature of the ground, as safe as from the howdah, but it is generally dangerous when the wounded tiger is followed on foot into the cover, where he has taken refuge, and it may be truly said, "Le jeu ne vaut pas la chandelle." Works on tiger-shooting in all its forms abound, and stirring incidents in the howdah and on foot are numerously recorded; it would seem like repeating an oft-told tale to tell of them again, but I shall conclude this history of the great cat, by relating a few anecdotes descriptive of his habits, and of the circumstances under which he is hunted and slain.

Tiger-shooting, though a less dangerous amusement than supposed by many, is not altogether exempt from peril, even when pursued, as it generally is, in Bengal, from elephants, for though the mahouts and the sportsmen in the howdah are rarely injured, accidents may occur, whilst the beaters and others on foot, who are in the vicinity of the hunted tiger, are occasionally wounded or killed. This mode of tiger shooting certainly combines sufficient of excitement with personal danger to make it interesting. On foot, it entails an amount of danger and risk of life, which I venture to think is hardly justifiable in a mere amusement, as many serious and fatal accidents only too clearly prove.

The following incidents, taken from a recent number of Allen's *Indian Mail* of 6th April, 1874, and the *Calcutta Englishman* of 24th April, 1874, are examples of the kind of danger that may occasionally occur in tiger-shooting from the howdah:—

"While antelope-shooting in the Dhoon, up got a tiger which was wounded. On being rapidly followed, tiger, elephant, and rider, all fell into a deep pit dug for catching wild elephants! The tiger crawled up by the elephant's head, and was shot in the act of clutching at the occupant of the howdah, and luckily managed only to claw him slightly, when he rolled over dead! A very narrow escape!"

"A rather curious tiger hunt, in which the tiger seemed to think that he should have his share of the sport, as well as the 'shikari,' occurred some short time ago in the Dhoon. A gentleman well known in

Dehra, an enthusiastic though rather inexperienced sportsman they say, went out about a month ago into the Eastern Dhoon for a day or two's shooting. Arrived on the ground, he was seated in his howdah on the elephant, looking out anxiously for game of some sort, when the mahout suddenly cried, 'Shér, Sahib,—burra Shér!' for a tiger had made his appearance unexpectedly close to the elephant. The gentleman hurriedly fired, and planted a ball from his rifle, not in the tiger's shoulder but in his abdomen. This mistake must have been due to surprise at the tiger's sudden advent on the scene, and the consequently hurried shot; otherwise such a want of knowledge of anatomy as was evinced in seeking a vital spot in the abdomen would be unpardonable. The consequences of the mistake were serious; for the tiger, resenting the sudden disturbance in the region, where the remains of his last kill were peacefully reposing, charged the elephant, and by a spring succeeded in planting his fore paws on her head, while his hind legs clawed and scratched vigorously for a footing on her trunk. Imagine the feelings of the mahout, with a tiger within six inches of his nose! the elephant trumpeting, shaking, and rolling with rage and pain, till he was barely able to maintain his seat on her neck at all; and the occupant of the howdah, too, tumbled from top to bottom, and from side to side of it, as if he were a solitary pill in a pillbox too large for him. Of course in this predicament he was utterly unable to use his rifle to rid the elephant of the unwelcome head-dress she was perforce wearing; the attempt to fire, in all that shaking, would probably have resulted in his blowing out the mahout's brains instead of the tiger's, or in his shooting himself. Meanwhile the mahout, with the courage of despair, slipped out the *gaddela* or cushion on which he sat, and, rolling it round his left arm, and taking the iron *gujbág* in his right, assailed the tiger manfully about the ears. But, being thickheaded, he did not seem to mind the *gujbág* at all; for, after taking a bite at the elephant's forehead, he calmly continued his struggles for a footing on the reluctant and ever-dodging trunk, heedless of the rain of blows on his thick skull, and no doubt promising himself to square accounts presently by swallowing the mahout, *gujbág*, and all. But the elephant was beginning to see that she couldn't shake the tiger off, so she tried another plan; and, making an extempore battering-ram of herself, with the tiger as a buffer, she charged straight at a sāl tree, thinking to make a tiger-pancake on the spot. But the sāl tree, alas! was a small one, and gave way under the shock, and away went tree, tiger, and elephant into an old and half filled up *obi*, or elephant-pit, which happened to be conveniently placed to receive them just on the other side of the fallen tree. The tiger and the mahout were both knocked off by the shock and fall; but the latter, luckily for himself, fell out of the pit, the former into it under the elephant. The elephant now had her share of the sport, and gave the tiger such a kicking while he lay under her, making a kind of shuttlecock of him between her fore and hind legs, that the breath must have been almost kicked out of him: then deeming she had done enough for honour and glory, and that she couldn't eat the tiger if she did kill him, she commenced climbing out of the pit, whose crumbled and sloping sides luckily made the scramble out practicable. The mahout, who had by this time picked himself and his scattered wits up, rushed round and caught her by the ear just as she reached the level, and was preparing for a bolt, and, scrambling rapidly up to his perch on her neck, succeeded in stopping her and turning her face to the foe once more. The elephant being now under command, our sportsman at length resumed his proper share in the proceedings, and the tiger being still at the bottom of the pit, breathless, if not senseless, from the kicking he had undergone, by a well-directed shot put him finally *hors-de-combat*, and had the satisfaction of carrying him into the station in triumph, where his skin is preserved as a witness of this strange tiger hunt. The elephant, though it got one nasty bite, and was badly scratched about the trunk and forelegs, is now none the worse for its single combat with the monarch of the Indian forests."

Despite his strength, and the ferocity with which he uses his formidable weapons when he is roused, it is remarkable how frequently men have escaped from his clutches. Numbers are now living who have been in the jaws, or have been struck down by the terrible forearm of the tiger, and yet have survived to tell the tale. Several such cases have occurred within my own knowledge.

Though the tiger frequently does not succumb until he has received many wounds, and will continue fighting to the last even when desperately injured—sometimes even springing up and seizing the elephant or man approaching his apparently lifeless body, and perhaps falling dead in his last efforts to charge—he not unfrequently falls to a single shot; I have seen this on several occasions, and on four or five have had the satisfaction of bagging the game with a single bullet from smooth-bore or rifle. A ball through the neck, if it cut the spinal cord, is instantly fatal, and the tiger turns a somersault and lies dead in his tracks. A ball through the lungs or heart, behind the shoulder or through the abdomen, near the spine, by cutting the aorta, will cause rapid death, and the tiger is found dead within a few yards of where he was struck. But it is remarkable how many bullets they will take in the head if the brain escape—as it often does, owing to the comparatively small size of the brain cavity—or in the abdomen, trunk, or limbs, without being disabled. Though mortally wounded they go on fighting, and may do much damage, or may even effect their escape.

For ordinary howdah shooting, the smooth twelve-bore for the average shots (which are at from 20 to 40 or 50 yards), with round or conical bullets, and three drachms of powder, is sufficient; for longer shots, or when on foot, the ordinary rifle or express is essential; but even for tigers the use of explosive shells is to be deprecated! A short double carbine breech-loader of large bore would be most useful, as would a pistol, either double-barrelled or on the revolver principle, carrying a large bullet, say of the bore of 8 or 10, according to the old round bullet gauge.

The following remarkable confirmation of the tiger's vitality, and the danger attending the pursuit on foot, is taken from a recent number of the *Indian Medical Gazette* (March 2nd, 1874):—

"On the 17th of January last, when beating for a supposed leopard, a fine tiger walked directly under the tree, on a low branch of which I was sitting, giving me a deliberate shot at a distance of not more than four feet. He dropped on the spot, clawed furiously at the ground, and turned round and round for about fifteen seconds, then pulled himself together, and set off at a gallop, getting my second shot after going about thirty yards. This turned him. He went about fifteen yards more in a series of wild plunges, and then fell over, gave a kick or two, and died. On examination he proved to be a male, 9 feet 7 inches (skin stretched to 11 feet 3 inches) in length. The ball, an ordinary twelve-bore round bullet, fired from a smooth bore with 3¼ drachms of No. 6 powder, had struck him about an inch to the right of the spine, passed through the right lung, struck the heart in the ventricular septum below the right auricle, and torn a huge hole through the right ventricle, besides opening the left into the right, then grazed the left lung and emerged below, an inch and a half to the left of the mesial line. The exit wound, both in the recent and in the dried skin, was very decidedly smaller than that of entrance, a phenomenon I have frequently observed both in men and animals. In the heart, however, the usual rule held good, and the aperture of exit was twice the size of that of entrance. I have frequently heard of such cases. A friend of mine tells me that he has seen a tiger go 150 yards with his heart 'blown to bits' by a shell; and a second assures me that another wounded as mine was, went 80 yards after attempting to pull him out of a tree. My second bullet entered behind the left elbow and the radius, or the beast might have gone further than it did. As it was, he went nearly fifty yards, and, although he died probably within a minute, it might have been a very awkward minute for me had he seen me. The moral of the case for sportsmen is—always aim at the brain." We might add also—do not shoot tigers on foot!

The following incidents, extracted from Indian papers, are interesting:—

"On Monday morning (the 13th) as two officers of H.M.'s 66th Regiment, Messrs. F. and C., were out in the jungles below Ramghat, above Sawunt Waree, and on the look-out for bison and bears, one of them was followed by a tiger, which scared the native shikarrie into a tree, leaving Mr. C. to face the growling brute. It advanced towards him by a bound or two, but as the hunter stood firm the game began to move off, and then incautiously placed itself on a rock, whereupon the sportsman accepted the invitation and gave him a bullet through the shoulder. This appears to have been a fatal shot, for the tiger gave a lurch forward and threw itself down a ravine, where, by blood stains, it was tracked by Mr. F. into a deep cavern. Having no beaters to assist nor lights to guide them, the hunters were obliged to leave their prey to die alone. The place where the incident occurred is nearly five miles north-west of the Ghat highway, and as the slain beast was a reputed man-eater, the few villagers who dwell in those mountain districts are well pleased because the sahibs got the tiger, instead of the tiger getting one of the sahibs, as he evidently intended to do."—*Times of India*, April 20th, 1874.

"The writer of 'Three Months in the Forests of Travankor' describes the following scene in the forest:—'Threading our way carefully, single file, along the narrow track, now cutting a path through the dense jungle with our hunting knives (essential appendages to an expedition such as ours), again getting to a clearer space where the fresh breezes fanned our heated brow, and glimpses of wooded hills and slopes and valleys appeared through the trees, but still proceeding steadily upwards, we at length came to an open space on the verge of a steep and precipitous hill side, where we sat down to rest and enjoy the beauty of the scene. On one hand towered the mighty forest trees rising tier above tier to the blue heavens; on the other, a yawning precipice sloped down to where a mountain torrent settled among great boulders of rock far below us. While we were gazing in quiet admiration of the scene, a rustling of the trees and sounds of hurried footsteps rapidly approaching, made us turn hastily round, and a magnificent sight greeted our astonished eyes. A noble stag, his antlers thrown back in act of listening, his nostrils dilated in terror, was flying down the path straight towards us, and in another instant the cause of his terror became apparent. A splendid tiger was following in his path, rushing down the narrow gorge, leaping over every obstacle that barred his way, and momentarily gaining on his prey. The stag flew on, not seeing us in his wild haste, until he was so close we could almost have touched him, when his terrified gaze fell upon us, standing rifle in hand, though we refrained from firing, seeing the tiger behind. To go on was death from our bullets, behind the tiger was close upon him, and without an instant's hesitation he turned and took a flying leap over the precipice, the tiger (who had never once caught sight of us, so intently was he gazing at his prey), following in his excitement, and in a moment both the noble animals were lost to sight among the branches of the trees, where they must have been dashed into a thousand pieces before they reached the bottom.' "—*Madras Mail.*

Some years ago Major A., a sportsman of great experience, skill, and resolution, when hunting with a companion, wounded a tiger in heavy tree-jungle. The animal remained in the cover crouching under a large branching tree. Major A.'s elephant became unsteady, probably from having been clawed by the tiger, and getting beyond the mahout's control ran away. This most dangerous of all accidents occurring among trees, was attended with the not unusual result—the howdah was crushed against an overhanging branch, and swept from the elephant's back. Major A. and the native in the khawas—that is the back seat of the howdah—were likewise swept away, but seizing the branch, hung suspended as the elephant passed from under them. The native being light and active swung himself on to the branch and was safe. Major A. not having so secure a hold, and probably not being so agile, was unable to do so, and after hanging suspended for a few moments, vainly attempting to get on to the branch, at length dropped to the ground, and, as ill luck would have it, fell on to the wounded tiger's back, which was lying under the tree. Being wounded in the spine the tiger was unable to move his hind-quarters, and could not rise, but retaining all his vigour in the fore part of the body and limbs, struck at and drew Major A. within his grip, and, infuriated with rage, wreaked his fury on the unfortunate gentleman; seizing him first by one leg he severely lacerated it, then leaving that, he seized the other, and bit it more severely. Major A. was utterly unable to get away from the infuriated animal, and spent some dreadful moments in this awful position. His companion, whose elephant had also taken fright, shortly after reappeared on the scene, and gave the wounded tiger the *coup de grâce*. Major A., frightfully wounded and exhausted by loss of blood, was then carried some distance into the nearest station, where it was found necessary to amputate one leg. Notwithstanding his serious injuries and the capital operation, he recovered, and has lived to return to England.

The case of Colonel H. has already been mentioned. A tigress at one bound, receiving a fatal wound as she sprang, reached the elephant's head, and seizing him, they came together to the ground. Though severely wounded, he survived the injuries for many years.

Major B., when shooting in Central India on foot, severely wounded a tiger, and though he retreated immediately to the trunk of a fallen tree, was seized by the arm by the infuriated brute, and dragged to the edge of a nullah, down which they both rolled into the stream at the bottom, where the tiger died, but not before it had inflicted such serious wounds as to render amputation of the limb necessary. This daring sportsman happily survives, and fills a high office under the Indian Government.

The late Colonel S., a most distinguished soldier and sportsman, when following a wounded tiger on foot in the long grass, was suddenly seized and carried off by the animal he was seeking. He managed, however, to effect his escape without having received any very serious injury, and rejoined his companion, who had deemed him lost.

Mr. ——, when out snipe shooting with some companions in Bengal, was informed by the natives of a village situated near a rice field, that some large animal was in the vicinity, which, from their description, they supposed to be a wolf. Mr. —— says that, as he was walking on the outskirts of the rice, which was full grown, he became suddenly aware of a tiger staring at him from among the rice, and in a moment he was struck down and seized by the shoulder. He was hardly able to remember what occurred or how he escaped; but he did escape, for the tiger, after giving him a severe shake, and having plunged his fangs into the shoulder, left him wounded and half senseless. He was carried home and recovered, after a long and exhausting illness, which resulted in permanent injury to the shoulder-joint and limb.

Mr. —— went after a tiger on foot in Lower Bengal, and wounded it. It had taken refuge in some light tree-cover, and was crouching under the trees. On being pointed out to him, he fired, this time with a shell, which exploded in the tiger's body, inflicting a most deadly wound; but notwithstanding, the brute had strength enough left to charge and seize him by the arm and shoulder, falling dead in the act of crushing the limb between his teeth. This gentleman recovered after protracted suffering, but with a stiffened and wasted limb.

The three following cases are extracted from a report by Dr. Downie, in the *Indian Medical Gazette* of December 2nd, 1872:—

Sowâr Bhart Singh, aged twenty-six, rajput, on 9th August, while acting as a beater, was attacked by a wounded tigress. His matchlock missed fire, he struck one blow on the head with his tulwâr, and was then knocked down. One of the officers with whom he had gone out, shot the tigress through the head while she was standing over the Sowâr. He was carried in fifteen miles, and I saw him at 10 o'clock p.m. There were about a dozen tooth wounds in the left forearm without fracture, one apparently penetrating into the wrist joint from behind. He had a scalp wound three quarters of an inch in length near the vertex, and a claw wound about one and a half inches long from the inner part of the left eyebrow skirting the orbit. Stitches of fine silver wire and cold applications were ordered.

There was also a compound fracture of the radius and ulna, just below the left elbow. There seemed no hope of saving the limb, but as no operative appliances were at hand, and the man was much exhausted by his journey, it was deemed right to wait till morning. The arm was secured by loops to a splint, and cold water applied. A grain of opium was given, to be repeated if necessary. He passed a tolerably easy night, and at 6 a.m. on the 10th there was a good deal of inflammatory swelling, and other mischief. In addition to several deep tooth wounds at and near the fracture, there were two or three above the elbow, with much bruising, inflammatory swelling, and emphysematous crepitation. Amputation was performed on the 23rd October. The wound healed.

Narain, camel driver, aged twenty-two, brought in on 8th September. Had been attacked by a tiger two days before. Had a deep wound just behind the upper part of the great trochanter, about three inches in depth, obliquely upwards; a flesh wound on outer front of thigh, about four inches long and one and a half inches broad. The wounds progressed favourably, though slowly. He recovered.

Buldeo Singh, rajput, aged thirty, on the evening of 22nd September, was brought in mauled by a wounded tiger. On the front of the left shoulder was a deep flesh wound, and on the back of the shoulder a superficial lacerated wound, two and a half inches by one inch. There were three fang wounds in the left flank; one in front, large enough to have admitted two fingers at least, penetrating into the abdomen; two wounds behind led down to the abdominal cavity, but did not injure the bowel. He had also one or two slight wounds over the ribs. Under cotton-wool, dipped in carbolic oil, the wounds rapidly healed; the man is now able to walk about, and there only remains a superficial wound, which is healing.

There is little to remark of these cases except the small constitutional disturbance.

The following have recently occurred :—

Near Roorkee, an officer fired at and wounded the tiger from a machàn, as it was seizing a buffalo. He followed on foot, and came on the tiger in the grass; fired as it charged, and mortally wounded the brute, which, however, had strength enough left to rush in and seize him by the shoulder, inflicting severe wounds. The tiger actually fell over dead, with his jaws closed on the officer's shoulder ;—the narrowest escape, with life, conceivable. This officer was placed on the sick list on the 4th April, 1874, having been injured on the 2nd of that month. The wounds were washed and ligatured in the jungle, prior to removal to Roorkee. On examination the shoulder was found greatly swollen, the ligatures so tense as to necessitate their division; in this condition it was found impossible accurately to diagnose the nature and extent of the injuries sustained. There were two extensive lacerated wounds on the front of the deltoid, and two corresponding to them on the dorsum scapulæ, produced doubtless by the fangs of the tiger. There was also a deep penetrating wound at the acromion, which extended deeper than the third joint of the forefinger. On the inner aspect of this wound the rough surface of the fractured acromion could be detected, while the outer fragment was dragged deep into the wound, and was only on one occasion touched by the finger. The spine of the scapula was fractured about its centre, and there were other less serious injuries of the back and leg, from the animal's claws. The nervous shock which followed this accident was excessive, and for about fifteen days the patient's mind was quite unsettled, his ideas wandering and disconnected; his eyes staring, tongue coated, pulse varying from 133, or fluttering with intermissions. Any attempt at fixing the limb aggravated the foregoing symptoms, and the idea was abandoned, position on pillows being substituted. The sloughing and discharge from the wounds was at first very great, but improvement manifested itself in this, as in all other respects, from about the twentieth day. The patient's limb continued powerless, but his general health and condition of mind daily improve. Treatment consisted in a thorough cleansing of the wounds with solution, permanganate of potash, and their subsequent treatment with carbolic oil. Bark and ammonia, in effervescence, with generous diet, prescribed daily.

Those who fall into the tiger's clutches do not always escape so fortunately, and were the cases of all sportsmen who have perished published, a long list would proclaim the dangers they incur.

Mr. K. was induced to follow a wounded tiger on foot on Saugur Island, where, in some low scrubby jungle, which barely reached his waist, he was suddenly attacked. The tiger had evidently been watching him, and rushing on him seized him by the knee, which was perforated by the fangs, and the bones much crushed. The tiger shook him violently several times. Mr. K.'s brother came to his aid, and wounded the tiger again, which then made off, leaving his victim helpless and bleeding on the ground. The case terminated fatally, after protracted suffering; this unfortunate gentleman, who would not submit to amputation, succumbed to the exhaustion produced by his wounds.

Some years ago, in the Madras Presidency, Captain H. went out after a tiger on foot. He was accompanied by beaters and a spaniel. The dog, when questing in the jungle, flushed a tiger, which endeavoured to escape. Captain H. got some shots, and wounded it more than once. It charged, and seized him by the loins on one side, gave him a fierce shake or two, dropped him, and then seizing him on the other side repeated the shaking and again dropping, left him and disappeared. His beaters had escaped up trees or elsewhere meanwhile, but when the tiger departed they came to his aid, and carried him into the station. He suffered no pain, and described how the tiger had seized and worried him. He sank from the shock and exhaustion, within a few hours.

Were the records of the Medical Board searched, no doubt several additions might be made to the above cases.

The following incident in tiger shooting from the howdah shows that the sport so pursued is not always unattended with danger:—

Some years ago, when in company with a party who were returning to camp, after a blank day in the Oude Terai, and when near the tents, towards sunset, a villager came up to the line of elephants, and said there were two tigers in a swamp near at hand, and that they had been causing great destruction among the cattle.

The sportsmen—there were only two—accordingly proceeded to the spot, and forming line with about twenty elephants, beat up the swamp. They had not proceeded far when one of the tigers was started, and was killed almost by the first shot. He was left lying where he fell, whilst the line beat on in pursuit of the other tiger, which had doubled back at the time the first was killed. The line was taken back, and again beat up the swamp—whilst so engaged one of the howdah elephants became much excited, and could not be persuaded to move on—giving evident signs of the vicinity of a tiger. This presently proved to be the dead one. The rest of the line meanwhile had passed on, and whilst the occupant of the howdah on the elephant that had been arrested by the dead tiger was looking down into the grass, to see the fallen tiger, he heard the shrill trumpeting of an alarmed elephant ahead, accompanied by a couple of shots, and immediately perceived that his companion's elephant, a few hundred yards ahead of him, had been seized by the other tiger, which was on its head. The elephant, from fright and pain, being nearly pulled to the ground, the occupant of the howdah managed with great difficulty to keep his seat—whilst holding on with one hand he contrived to fire two shots with the other. This, with the shaking of the elephant, which was much agitated, dislodged the tigress, which crouched on the ground, her eyes glaring, and was preparing for another spring, when No. 2 came up, and gave her the *coup de grâce.* In this case the occupant of the howdah had the narrowest escape of being thrown out on to the enraged and wounded tigress.

The following extracts are from a Journal kept during a tiger-shooting expedition to the Oude Terai, in 1855, *before the Mutiny, and previous to the Annexation of Oude :—*

"*March* 19*th*, 1855.—We made our first entry into the forest, a small part of the edge of which we had to cross to arrive at a grassy plain on the opposite bank of the Girwah, where the tigers had been seen; and on approaching the bank of the river we passed over some recent footprints.

"The outskirts of the forest are not dense, and consist of the Sisoo—(Dalbergia sisoo), dâk (Butea frondosa), catechu (Khair mimosa), semel

(Bombax), and other trees. There are numerous open glades covered with long grass, in which both the spotted deer (Cervus axis) and the hog deer (Cervus porcinus) are found.

"We beat all over the plain but found no tigers. They had been there, but were from home; and, re-crossing the Girwah, we returned, making a short detour through the edge of the forest to a large swamp about a mile to the westward of the place where we had entered the forest. We sent the whole line in, and the elephants were immediately hidden in the long nurkool grass. I and H. took the plain side, B. and D. the opposite side close to the edge of the forest, keeping a little in advance of the line that was crashing and tearing through the nurkool behind us.

"When the elephants had got about a quarter of the way through the swamp, some of them began to trumpet and show other signs of uneasiness. A moment afterwards two tigers broke cover, bounding out into the plain within thirty or forty yards of my elephant; fifty yards further on they entered the jungle again. The moment my elephant saw them she turned sharp round with a scream and bolted, fortunately for me, across the plain; had it been into the forest I was done for. The mahout stopped her in about three minutes, and back we came to the edge of the swamp. I now took up my station at an opening in the long grass, where, being driven before the elephants, it was evident they must cross. H. this time took up his position close to me; my elephant again became very restive, uneasy, and alarmed. The elephants in the swamp again gave signs that the tigers were near, and in a moment, within forty yards of us, a large male tiger bounded across the opening and plunged into the jungle on the opposite side. Off went my elephant again as before, this time taking H.'s elephant with her, to our disgust. We had just time to get a couple of hurried shots at him as he entered the swamp before our elephants were off with us. We stopped them as before, and came back to the head of the swamp into which the big tiger had just crossed, and waited there for him as the line beat up behind; we heard his foot-falls as he came along before the line, but when he saw that he was near the end, and I suppose distrusting the plain, he suddenly turned back and charged through the line; we turned immediately, and just as we got back to the opening where he had before crossed, he again broke cover and bounded across the opening, trying to make for the high bank on the opposite side. H. got first shot, being a little in front of me, and rolled him over with a ball through his back. We pushed up to where he was howling and struggling in the long grass—a magnificent sight—and emptied our barrels into him. We left him lying stiff and dead to go after the other tiger, which had also doubled back, and whilst we were shooting his companion had broken cover and was cantering across the plain. We were off after him as quickly as possible, the race who should be first. B. came up with him in the long grass and rolled him over. He picked himself up immediately, and made a charge right at the elephants. B. gave him another shot. I also gave him a couple of barrels, and he was secured; just as I fired he was close under the elephants, his eyes glaring, mouth open, ears well back, looking awfully wicked and determined, but he was too much crippled by B.'s shot to spring. My elephant again made an attempt to bolt, but this time was not so bad, only going a few yards; by the time I got back to the spot the tiger was dead. We padded them, and returned to our camp, which was pitched at a dreary, desolate-looking spot, called Chelhua, not more than two or three miles from the old ground, being only just across the plain on the opposite side of the river. After dinner we skinned and measured the tigers by candle-light. The big one as he lay, before the skin was taken off, was 9 feet 5 inches; the small one 8 feet."

"*March 20th.*—We entered the forest for a short distance, and before noon had padded a beautiful full-grown tigress. We beat her out of a small bhagar (swamp). She broke cover a long way ahead of us, and concealed herself in the long grass in an open plain, where we came up with her. B. got the first shot at her. Off she went again, we all following as hard as piadahs and moogries could make the elephants go. Suddenly I saw D.'s elephant stop, and immediately afterwards sink down on her knees. The tigress had charged home and got her by the trunk. The elephant, Raj Kawan, was very staunch, and the tigress was very soon knocked and shaken off without doing any mischief. Just as I approached the spot she charged, and received two balls as she was hugging the elephant by the fore leg, which brought her down again. She made another attempt to charge, but without success, and she received the contents of five or six more barrels before she died. She remained in the crouching posture, as if ready for a spring, and it was a moment or two before we were certain that she was dead. She was a very beautifully-marked full-grown tigress, of what the natives call the Keerie variety. She fought and died hard. The natives have the idea, and many Europeans share it with them, that there are two varieties of tiger, the Keerie and Tinger; but they are mistaken, there is only one, and any difference as to colour, size, or shape, is mainly what depends on age, sex, and local causes. Some tigers are much more beautifully marked than others. Those that frequent the forest much are said to be darker and more vividly marked than the others, but this is the only real difference. My authority for this is a good one —Mr. Blyth, of the Asiatic Society's Museum in Calcutta.

"The elephant was not in the least injured by the tigress, and we, especially D., are much pleased with her. She is not the one that ran away the other day with him; he had discarded her, and selected this one from amongst the beaters, on account of her size. She is very rough, and quite unfit for carrying a howdah, but in tiger-shooting steadiness is an invaluable merit in an elephant, and one that covers a multitude of sins. She stood beautifully when the tigress charged, and seemed to be perfectly fearless and indifferent, whilst many of the pad elephants had bolted and were rushing about in all directions but that of the tiger. I was on H.'s elephant, a very fine animal, perfectly fearless, but a little unsteady; when the tigress charged, she snorted and kicked the ground, and would have rushed at the animal had she been allowed. We sent a pad back with the tigress, and went on beating for another which had been recently seen in the neighbourhood, but though we looked hard we could not succeed. We tried several most likely-looking places in the forest, and then crossed the old bed of the Cowriallie, to a chur covered with long grass, our shikarrie insisting that it was a likely find, but we were again unfortunate, for we found nothing in the grass but peacocks and hog deer. We found the river running in a new channel on the other side of the chur, a beautiful clear stream with a sandy bottom. In crossing the old bed of the river we came upon one or two quicksands, and in one of them 'Shamguttah' again stuck fast, but after wallowing, struggling, and rolling in the ooze for some time she extricated herself.

"We had very little small game shooting this day, being constantly on the look-out for tigers. D. knocked over a pig and a hog deer. B. shot a nurkool partridge. I had also a long shot at a herd of spotted deer, but they were too far off. On returning to the tents at 5 P.M., we found the tigress skinned and the flesh already picked off her bones by innumerable vultures and jackals. Her skin was full of bullet holes, but was most beautifully marked."

"*March 22nd.*—Started at about 10 A.M., and tried part of the ground we had gone over yesterday.

"Our shikarrie took us to a recent 'kill.' The buffalo, for such it was, was very little injured, only a small piece of the hind quarter having been eaten. The place was perfect—a beautiful glade in the forest with a very long and dense nurkool swamp on the border of which he had killed. We beat right through it, but could not find the tiger. He had been disturbed by the aheers, and had most probably retreated into the forest, which is close at hand, very dense, and surrounding the glade and swamp completely. We were told that the aheers had driven him off the 'kill' that very morning.

"We then proceeded to beat out another very long and deep swamp with steeply wooded banks, along which we had much difficulty in conducting our elephants. Just as we arrived at the extreme end of the swamp, and fortunately on the side on which B. and I were waiting, looking at the line crashing and floundering along through the nurkool and water, suddenly, with the usual two short roars or grunts, out sprang a large male tiger. We both had snap shots at him. As he came at us B. turned him right at me. My two barrels, the contents of one of which he received in the hip, turned him again across the swamp, and then, as he was rushing up the steep bank on the opposite side, he came face to face with H. and D., who shot him dead as he charged up amongst the trees.

"I measured him; he was 10 feet 1 inch, as he lay dead on the spot where he was shot. His skin when taken off was over 11 feet. All say he is one of the finest tigers they have seen. He had evidently been sneaking along quietly before the line, hoping to get into the forest at some favourite opening, but we followed too close for that, and when at last he was forced to break cover in the open, he did what tigers do not often do I am told, charged right at us, though unwounded."

"*March 23rd.*—Recrossed the river this morning at the same place as yesterday, and made for the "kill" of which we had received information the previous evening; but, though we found the remains of the cow, the tiger was not there. We pushed on to a patch of long grass jungle, in an open country, here and there interspersed with trees, and as the beaters entered one end, the tiger broke cover from the other, and bolted across the plain towards a ridge of high ground with some tree jungle and a swamp at the other side of the ridge. We followed as hard as we could make the elephants go, the mahouts hammering them on the head with the ancus (hook) and the piadahs (footmen) on the tail with the moogries. We came up to the swamp in about five or six minutes, and, forming line, beat right up it. It was not very deep on the side I took with H. and D., the opposite one to the trees, but near the trees the water was very deep, as we afterwards found.

"B. remained on the ridge to receive the tiger did he get up the hill after breaking cover. We moved steadily on, and out he came with the usual two roars. I was fortunate in getting the first shot at about forty yards distant. The ball struck him in the neck, and without a struggle he rolled over, dead. We pushed up, and found him floating; the ball had struck just as he was entering the deep water to make for the bank where B. was waiting. We dragged him out, and found that it was a fine, full-grown tigress, very prettily marked. We sent her off to camp at once to be skinned, and went on in the direction of another swamp not far ahead. The Muèla swamp is very extensive—one of the real primeval productions of nature—and dismal, wild, and gloomy it looks; but, as it turned out, a rare cover for tigers. The water in the centre for great part of its length is deep and dark; large alligators and strange-looking fish make their appear-

* The moogrie is a club with sharp spikes in it.

ance on its surface, and quietly disappear when they perceive the strange objects on the banks. The edges of the swamp are covered with long and dense grass and trees; on the left-hand side, where we approached it, the forest itself is dense and magnificent, the branches of the trees overhanging the gloomy, treacherous-looking water below, and the thick grass and tangled low jungle which encroaches equally on both forest and water.

"This cover is a favourite haunt of tigers, pythons, and alligators. B., who was on the forest side, shot a large python, that glided quietly away with a bullet through his sinuous body, into the shelter of some impenetrable jungle, just as I fired at a large alligator which was lying quietly on the surface of the water, with the end of his nose and eyes only appearing above the surface. The ball struck him in the head, and he quietly sunk to the bottom, a few bubbles of air slowly rising to the surface, only remaining to indicate where he had been.

"We had a line of twenty-four elephants to-day; the rajah was with us, and had with him four or five of his own. We divided the elephants into two divisions, one half with B. and the rajah on the forest side, the other half with H. D. and myself on the other. We had not proceeded far before a number of Lungoor monkeys (entellus), which were bounding about in the trees on B.'s side, suddenly began to screech and spring violently forward, shaking the branches of the large trees like the passage of a whirlwind through them. It was evident that they had seen something that alarmed them seriously. In a minute more I heard the cry of 'Bagh, bagh.' A large tiger had gone out before B., and was concealed in the grass somewhere ahead of us; the monkeys had seen him, and gave the alarm.

"We got him after a hard chase. He was shot in a large clump of nurkool grass in which he took refuge, and from which he would not break. The ground was too heavy for the elephants to go in, and the anars we threw in would not burn on account of the water. We heard, though we could not see him, and by the moving of the grass we could see his whereabouts. We kept firing volleys in upon him, and B. got a momentary glimpse which he took advantage of to give him a shot through the back, which appeared to quiet him, for the grass ceased to move.

"After waiting a minute, H.'s khas burdars went into the jungle sword in hand, and dragged him out through the mud and water, quite dead.

"We now got out of our howdahs and had tiffin under a tree, whilst the men were padding the tiger. After a short rest we mounted and proceeded along the swamp, which now altered in character, the deep water ceasing and a mixture of long grass, nurkool and kulwa, stretching right across it, with trees of the willow and wild jamun interspersed at intervals. The elephants formed line again across the swamp, and within ten minutes we put up another large tiger. He broke cover into an opening in the swamp, and it was magnificent to see him look round as if astonished at the noise and confusion in this usually quiet and secluded spot. As he saw us he received our bullets, which wounded and infuriated him, for up he came right at D. and H.'s elephants, who were a little in advance of mine. The next shots turned him, and he made off in a direction ahead of us up the swamp (amongst the trees), which here takes a bend. We followed as quickly as possible, for the trees on the bank were here thickly clustered together; by going higher up on the bank I managed to get ahead, and in a few minutes I knew from the agitation of my elephant that I was near him. On looking down into the swamp there he was lying completely exposed under a tree at about forty yards from me, and how magnificent he looked with his ears well back, his eyes glaring, and back arched up ready for a charge! I took as steady an aim as I could, for my elephant was much excited, kicking the ground and shaking the howdah dreadfully, and fired; to my horror the gun exploded with a report little louder than that of a common percussion cap. I tried the second barrel— it did the same; the tiger was now charging up the hill at my elephant. I seized a second gun, abusing the chuprassey in the khawas for having forgotten the bullets, as I thought was the case in his excitement, and pulled the triggers of both barrels; the result was the same—the powder was bad. The tiger was now close on my elephant, when D. and H. to my left hit him hard and turned him in their direction; as he went along the bank D. rolled him over like a hare with a bullet through the back. He picked himself up and staggered down into the bottom of the ravine, where we all followed and emptied our barrels into him. It was beautiful to see him roll over; but I almost pitied the brute as he staggered down the side of the ravine, and saw him crouching in the agonies of death, game to the last, and glaring savagely at us as he received the *coup de grâce*. We left him lying there, for in the meantime another tiger had been put up and seen by B. on the other side. I now examined into the cause of my gun's misfortune, and found that the chuprassey had just commenced a new flask of Pigou's powder, which had been either damp or was bad from age. I loaded three or four barrels with it, and found that it did exactly the same each time; it exploded, but with almost no report, and with barely force enough to send the bullet out of the gun. On examining the grains of powder I found that they had lost the shiny glazy appearance of good powder, and were agglomerated together in little lumps. This was one of the lessons a sportsman has to learn—look to your powder! The same mishap will not, I think, occur to me again.

"I found that another new flask which I opened was as bad, but fortunately I had a good one in the howdah, and in the meantime had borrowed a flask from H., and off we went after number four. After some beating we bagged him also, but not before he had been on one of the pad elephant's heads; the elephant was small, and being deep in the swamp, and coming suddenly on the tiger he was seized by the head. The tiger was, however, soon shaken off, and very soon after B. and the rajah on the other side killed him. The elephant's head was not much injured; there were two rather deep wounds, but they were not serious. The khas burdar behind the mahout fired at the tiger when on the elephant's head, but I don't believe he hit him. This is the fourth full-grown tiger to-day. Another was seen by B. to cross the swamp and get away into the forest on the side on which he was shooting. As we were a long way from home and had the rapids to cross, we set off for camp, not having time to beat for more to-day, but shall return to-morrow to make further discoveries in this magnificent swamp. It was a fine sight, our line of twenty-four elephants, with the grim monsters hanging across their backs, and really repaid one for all the hard work and sun, etc., to which we had been exposed."

"*March 24th.*—After breakfast this morning we again crossed the river at the same place and went straight to our yesterday's beat, where we got the three tigers, to try that part of it that was left unbeaten yesterday. We were again fortunate, for we found a magnificent tigress with two half-grown cubs, only a little beyond the place where yesterday we left off beating. We started her in the nurkool. She cantered on with the cubs into a broad open space covered with long grass on dry ground, and there came to bay. It was a beautiful sight to see her charging out at the line of elephants, whilst the cubs were running about in different directions, and each time being received and turned by a volley from the howdahs. At last she ceased to charge, but we saw the grass moving and heard her growling. We went up to the spot, and another barrel or two made her ours.

"In the meantime some of us went after the cubs, who were charging here and there in the grass, evidently in great fear and anxiety about their mother. They ran the gauntlet of some dozens of shots, and one got away into the forest badly wounded and bleeding at the mouth. As I was following him I came upon the other, who charged like a full-grown tiger; I pointed my gun downwards, and sent a bullet through his chest as he was grasping the elephant round the leg. This gave him his quietus, and I followed the other cub that had disappeared in the forest. I could not overtake him, and returned to the spot where the tigress was being padded. She was a beautiful creature, light, lean, active, and vicious, and seemed determined to do mischief. The aheers (cowherds) who took us to the place, said they had often watched her feeding the cubs and teaching them to hunt and kill. The piece of ground where we killed her was covered with the remains of cows, deer, etc.; as, indeed, all along and in the swamp we had observed the same. In fact, this seems to have been a most favourite stronghold for them."

"*March 27th.*—We did not get the tigress after all, though we found her traces in the swamp, in the shape of a newly-killed, almost warm, cow. She had heard us coming and sneaked off into the forest, which is dense on either side, and where there would not be the slightest chance of finding her. We therefore gave her up with reluctance, and struck off due westwards, towards a large swamp near Hilowna Gowrie, where we are to pitch our tents to-night. We were more successful here, for we got a very fine tiger in the swamp. We hardly expected to have got anything in it, for it looked more like a large Jheel than a Bhagar. The grass was short, and in many places there was really no cover at all. We put up quantities of partridges, snipe, painted snipe, and hog deer, and I was preparing to have a shot at the next partridge that rose, when suddenly I heard two or three shots to my left, and in another moment the well-remembered growls of a wounded and angry tiger. D. and B. had put him out of a clump of long grass and sent him over to H.

and me; we had an open space, with about a foot deep of water, between us. He charged us in the most determined manner, and was almost on my elephant when a couple of shots in the ribs turned him, and he went growling off to a clump of grass, in which he lay down. We went up, but before finishing him he had been on B.'s elephant's hind quarters. D., I think, gave him the *coup de grâce* in that position. He was a very fine tiger, and the aheers told us he had only just come from the forest, which was close to the swamp, to kill. He was lean and hungry looking, and had an old festering wound on one of his fore legs, and was also blind of an eye. He was 9 feet 7 inches in length. The aheers said that they had frightened him off a buffalo that he had struck down yesterday. He must have been awfully hungry and very savage. He would have killed again that day to a certainty. Where we entered the swamp, though it was beautiful grazing ground, the short, young, green grass being such as is much liked by cattle, there was not a single cow or buffalo in it. As we came out with the tiger on an elephant's back, we met the cattle going in in numbers. It is wonderful how instinct seems to tell them of the presence of their enemy. The number of cattle killed by tigers in the Terai annually must be enormous; they prefer them to any other food, for they give less trouble than deer and make a better meal. I suppose a tiger kills every third or fourth day, and when one or two establish themselves near a cattle-grazing village they very soon decimate the herd. They rarely attack men, and when they do so it is only when provoked. Some are man-eaters, but we met none such. I think from what I have seen and heard that they often show the most extraordinary forbearance, for already we have met with two men who have been in the grip of a tiger, and yet were allowed to go away almost unhurt.

"I believe that a tiger would seldom touch a man unless he went out of his way to disturb him, or he were very hard pressed by hunger. They nearly always try to get away when first found; but wound them, and they fight like devils incarnate! On returning to the tents, we found that the tiger had more than one old wound besides that in his fore leg, and whilst his skin was being taken off, a Bun-jarah came forward and told us that fifteen days ago his brother-in-law was returning from the forest in that direction; that in the dusk he saw something lying in the grass, as he forced his way through it, which he took to be a deer. He fired, and in the next moment, to his horror, he was in the grip of a large tiger. The animal seized him by the shoulder, but dropped him again almost immediately, and leaving him disappeared in the forest. The man is now recovering from the wounds, which do not appear from the description to have been very severe. It seems extraordinary that the tiger being wounded should have let him off so easily.

"After bagging our tiger we struck off through the edge of the forest in a northerly direction for a plain in the forest, in which there is said to be a good find. It is here that the tigress and cubs live. We beat it through, finding only long grass and a dry nullah, but got nothing except some hog deer. It was too dry for a tiger. We killed a little small game on our way back to the tents, and saw some florican, but as yet have not had a chance of getting a shot at this bird. The florican is an easy bird to shoot if you get down from your elephant and stalk him, but not otherwise. . . . .

"*April* 1st.—The weather was now beginning to get hot, and shortly after we returned to Lucknow."

Extracts from a Journal kept during a shooting expedition in Bengal, Ulwar, and the Nepaul Terai, in the year 1870.

"*January* 12*th.*—The party started after breakfast, and rode about eight miles, when they found about thirty elephants waiting at the village of Dobri. Having got into the howdahs, they proceeded to beat over the extensive nul and putiah jungle of Serajpore. After beating for some time, a young tigress was found. She made a charge along the line, but could neither make it good, nor could she break the line, and soon fell before the fire from the numerous howdahs of which she tried to run the gauntlet. H.R.H. had a good shot at her, and a shell from his rifle produced a marked effect. She was scarcely padded before a second tiger was afoot, close to where the first was killed. The line was taken back to beat up the ground again, and No. 2 was soon *hors-de-combât;* it proved to be a second tigress, somewhat larger than the first. The ryots of the neighbouring station were much pleased, for they had been losing many cattle lately, and the death of the two tigresses promised them some relief. A short beat was then made through a neighbouring patch of long grass jungle, but without success. After tiffin the party went along the picturesque road which leads to the ancient city of Gour; and after inspecting the interesting ruin of the Sona Musjid, branched off across the swamps towards the camp, which had left Turtipore and was pitched at Sookerbarri.

"*January* 13*th.*—Left camp after breakfast, and rode about three miles to the Mahanuddie. The elephants and howdahs had been sent on, and had crossed the river. At about eleven the beat commenced with a line of about forty-five elephants, over the extensive grassy undulating plains that abound in these parts of Malda, a district characterized by its picturesque groups of magnificent trees, chiefly of the Indian fig tribe. The line having been formed, it beat steadily on; very little game was seen, excepting a few black partridges and an occasional hog-deer or hare, when suddenly a signal went along the line that a tiger was afoot, and soon after he was seen bounding along with his tail in the air—making for a nullah several hundred yards ahead. He got up close under H.R.H.'s elephant, which was in the centre of the line; a few shots were fired, but apparently without effect, and H.R.H. lost the chance by having his shot gun in his hand at the time, and before he could change it the tiger was too far ahead. Making for the nullah, which was in one part clear of jungle, he was seen to wade across the nullah and enter the cover, but he was too far off to make it desirable to fire, as in the boundless plain of grass there was every chance of losing him if missed. As he appeared to be secure in its shelter, all waited for the line to come up; but he had meanwhile made off, and, though the nullah and grass were carefully beat, he was not seen again. This proved how true it is that the cold season, when the plains are covered with long grass, is not the season for tiger shooting. Had it been two months later, and the cover all burned, he would no doubt have been bagged. It is satisfactory to know that he remained there for any sportsman who might come that way in March or April." . . . . .

From Another Expedition, in Ulwar.

"*February 20th.*—It was intended to halt to-day,

and the party walked out to see the lake and the aqueducts of Silisere. A large alligator was wounded, but, the water being deep, it made its escape, although a man followed and drove a spear into it. News came from the Maharajah about 2 P.M. that a tiger had been found not very far off, and that it was being watched and surrounded to prevent its escape. The elephants were immediately sent on, and after tiffin the party rode out to the place where the tiger had been seen. The elephants were assembled in a hollow between two hills, and the tiger was said to be in a ravine on the hillside, about 600 to 800 feet high. As it was impossible to get at him on the elephants, it was determined to attack on foot, and accordingly some climbed the hill on one side of the ravine, which was full of thorny shrubs and broken masses of stone, whilst the rest took the other side. The shikarries and beaters, with several couples of dogs, that in appearance were something between a greyhound and a mastiff, were ranged on either side. After a long and fatiguing climb, each having taken his post, the sport commenced. A shot from H.R.H. set the tiger in motion, and, breaking cover, he ran the gauntlet of several guns. Making across the ravine he was turned, and when severely wounded went down the ravine towards the plain; all followed, and gradually closed in on him. He was not seen for a little time, and it was supposed that he was dead; but it was not so. He was soon in motion again, and, after charging, turned and went roaring down the ravine. He was again quiet for a moment, and then rushed out and charged C., whose rifle missed fire. The dogs were fortunately loosed at this critical moment, and, rushing in, turned him when within a few feet of C. The tiger was badly injured, having a broken foreleg, with other wounds. He got back into the ravine, the dogs going in and tugging vigorously at him in all directions. He knocked over several, but did not kill any. All closed in on him, and after a few more shots he was *hors-de-combât*. He turned out to be a fine male tiger. An elephant was left to pad and bring him into camp." . . . .

From an Expedition in the Oude Terai.

"*February 26th*, 1871.—The Maharajah crossed the river, and came into the camp, bringing with him some of his men, who exhibited their skill in cutting pieces of green wood with the kookrie. Soon afterwards the party got into their howdahs, and the usual beat in line with the elephants commenced. The beat lay again through grassy plains and forest, consisting chiefly of sul and ebony. The Mohân was recrossed, and the tents were in sight, when a Goorkah came up, and said he had just seen a tiger kill a cow. The cover was perfect, the country wild and uncultivated, long grass by the river side, and clumps of forest scattered here and there. The howdahs and pads were gradually got into line on the receipt of this welcome news, and the spot, a most tigerish one, gradually enclosed by a circle of elephants. The tiger was soon afoot, and received a shot from H.R.H.'s rifle. He made several attempts to break the line, but the elephants were staunch, and after some ineffectual charges he fell riddled with many bullets. He proved to be a fine male tiger, 10 feet 3 inches in length. He made little fight, for he had no chance of doing so. Several peacocks were in the grass at the time, and being so confused that they could not escape, were caught by the mahouts and charcuttahs, who picked them up. After this unexpected piece of luck, the line moved on to the new camp at Pursooah, about eight miles from the last, and in a plain about one mile from the Mohân. The Maharajah is encamped close at hand. The bag to-day consisted of the tiger, and about a dozen spotted and hog deer, hares, partridges, and peafowl. . . . . .

"*March 2nd.*—After breakfast the party set off for the jungle. The beat commenced in a 'khair' (Catechu) forest, and long grass; and soon the line was agitated from end to end, by the report that three tigers (a tigress and two full-grown cubs) were afoot. They soon made their appearance, and broke cover in fine style. One cub took to the left of the line, and was killed immediately. The others got away, and were lost in the forest. After a long beat in the forest, by the side of a nullah, and through a nurkool swamp, where nilgye, spotted deer, and other game in abundance were seen, the search was abandoned, and a general beat commenced, during which a fair amount of game was bagged, among others, an enormous python. It was so heavy that it required six or eight men to lift it on to the pad elephant. The line now beat on in an opposite direction, through the forest. The firing was pretty brisk, and the line had crossed to the other side of the patch of forest, when one of the pad elephants suddenly put up a small tiger, which bounded into the open, and crossed the plain. It was thought by some that a tigress was seen at the same time. For a moment he was lost sight of, but after a long stampede across the plain, during which time he had doubled back into a patch of long grass among a herd of tame buffaloes, by whom he got considerably knocked about, he was overtaken and killed by many shots. A patch of mud, in which he got entangled, was his destruction, as it prevented his escape to the forest, and allowed the elephants to come up. He tried to fight, but in vain, and fell, riddled with bullets. This was evidently one of the cubs seen in the morning. The first was 6 feet 6 inches, and the second 6 feet 9 inches long. The camp soon after this returned to the station.

TIGER

TIGER AND KILL

When the tiger has killed his prey, he drags it into cover to devour at his leisure. After eating, he lies up near it to protect the remains from marauding hyenas, jackals, and vultures.

THE GREAT LHONA TIGER

This is from the stuffed head of a monster of his kind.

Drawn by E. Caldwell. Swan Electric Engraving C°.

Tiger

Drawn by E. Caldwell. Swan Electric Engraving Co.

Tiger

1. Indian Lion.

2. Bengal Tiger.

4. Persian Leopard.

3. Indian Leopard.

5. Snow-Leopard.

6, Clouded Leopard.

7, Fishing-Cat.

8, Leopard-Cat.

9. Jungle-Cat.